Cincinnati Reds 2019

A Baseball Companion

Edited by Patrick Dubuque, Aaron Gleeman and Bret Sayre

Baseball Prospectus

Craig Brown and Dave Pease, Consultant Editors
Rob McQuown and Harry Pavlidis, Statistics Editors

Copyright © 2019 by DIY Baseball, LLC.
All rights reserved

This book or any part thereof may not be reproduced or transmitted in any form or by any means, electronic or mechanical, including photocopying, recording, or by any information storage and retrieval system, without permission in writing from the publisher.

Limit of Liability/Disclaimer of Warranty: While the publisher and the author have used their best efforts in preparing this book, they make no representations or warranties with respect to the accuracy or completeness of the contents of this book and specifically disclaim any implied warranties of merchantability or fitness for a particular purpose. No warranty may be created or extended by sales representatives or written sales materials. The advice and strategies contained herein may not be suitable for your situation. You should consult with a professional where appropriate. Neither the publisher nor the author shall be liable for any loss of profit or any other commercial damages, including but not limited to special, incidental, consequential, or other damages.

Library of Congress Cataloging-in-Publication Data:
paperback
ISBN-13: 978-1-949332-36-0

Project Credits
Cover Design: Kathleen Dyson
Interior Design and Production: Jeff Pease, Dave Pease
Layout: Jeff Pease, Dave Pease

Baseball icon courtesy of Uberux, from https://www.shareicon.net/author/uberux

Ballpark diagram courtesy of Lou Spirito/THIRTY81 Project, https://thirty81project.com/

Manufactured in the United States of America
10 9 8 7 6 5 4 3 2 1

Table of Contents

Foreword v
    Rob Mains

Statistical Introduction vii

Part 1: Team Analysis

Table for Two: Previewing the 2019 Cincinnati Reds 3
    Roger Cormier and Nicholas Zettel

Performance Graphs 9

2018 Team Performance 10

2019 Team Projections 11

Team Personnel 12

Great American Ball Park Stats 13

Reds Team Analysis 15

Part 2: Player Analysis

Reds Player Analysis 22

Reds Prospects 103

Part 3: Featured Articles

The Hole in The Shift is Fixing Itself 115
    Russell Carleton

The State of the Quality Start 119
    Rob Mains

Heads-Up Hacking—The First Pitch 125
    Matthew Trueblood

A Hymn for the Index Stat 131
    Patrick Dubuque

Index of Names 135

Foreword

Rob Mains

Welcome to this companion of the 2019 Cincinnati Reds. We at Baseball Prospectus are excited to provide this analysis of the Reds.

Our website, Baseball Prospectus, is a leader in delivering high-quality commentary and data to baseball fans everywhere. To some, those words—commentary and data—appear mutually exclusive. There are people out there who believe that traditional analysis and advanced analytics must run on different paths. But the simplistic narrative of stats vs. traditionalists just isn't true. Every team's analytics department interacts with scouting, development, and major league operations with a common goal: Delivering a championship. New technologies, like radar tracking of pitch speeds and movement, enable talent evaluators to focus on qualitative aspects of pitching like mechanics and pitch sequencing. In-game strategies like infield shifts, based on batters' hit tendencies, help turn balls in play into outs. Hitters use information to adjust their swings to maximize run production.

All these numbers can seem, at best, intimidating, and at worst, counterproductive to the casual fan. Even as technology and analysis have embedded themselves deeply into the way teams run, it can often feel like statistics create a displacement between the viewer and the sport, breaking them out of the action. And yet every fan incorporates the numbers to some degree; stats like batting average and earned run average, so fundamental to how we talk about performance, are actually complicated formulas. They don't bother people because those formulas have become second nature, as easy to translate as the action on the field.

Along the way, new statistics have entered baseball's lexicon. You'll see some of them, like on-base percentage (which measures a batter's ability to get on base via walk, hit batter, or hit), OPS (on-base plus slugging), and average exit velocity (the speed of balls off a hitter's bat) on broadcasts. Others, like DRC+, might well be new to you. Some of them have been well-defined to the public, others haven't. That lack of context has created ambiguity. Fans know that a ball hit 100 mph is scorched, but does that mean extra bases? (Not if it's hit on the ground or high in the air it doesn't.)

For those who are amenable to them, the new statistics can increase the enjoyment and understanding of the game. They can help fans identify when a pitcher is tiring, when a stolen base or a bunt attempt makes sense (and, more often, when it doesn't), or how a team's lineup might be constructed. Websites like Baseball Prospectus add to that understanding by weaving metrics into the narrative of the game. That's the goal of this publication: to take some of the newer, more complicated statistics and make them as intuitive as the ones on the back of old baseball cards.

But you don't need to love analytics to love baseball. The fans at BP who worked together to write this guide are captivated first and foremost by the game itself. We're drawn to Aaron Judge's power, Francisco Lindor's glove, Billy Hamilton's speed and Patrick Corbin's slider and don't need numbers to tell us why they're so mesmerizing. The underlying statistics provide depth to the game that we all love.

We hope you'll find that this guide helps you better understand the Reds. Our analysts have studied the team's major league personnel and its minor league affiliates to identify their strengths and weaknesses, both the obvious ones and those that only a careful dissection of players' performances—yes, including the data—can reveal. You don't need us to tell you who was good and who wasn't in 2018, but our models and writers can help you project how each player is going to perform this year and beyond, and appreciate the greatness of each new game as it unfolds. As in the sport itself, the human and analytic components combine to generate a deeper overall understanding.

Think back to the first time you saw a baseball game on a high-definition TV. You'd grown familiar with how the game looked and felt on a picture tube. But new TV allowed you to see details that you'd never seen before. That's how advanced statistics work. The game itself is why you're here and why you're buying this. (And, for that matter, why we wrote it.) The statistical measures provide the sharper focus, the detail, the depth of knowledge that you didn't have before, generating an overall superior picture. Enjoy the view.

—*Rob Mains is an author of Baseball Prospectus.*

Statistical Introduction

Sports are, fundamentally, a blend of athletic endeavor and storytelling. Baseball, like any other sport, tells its stories in so many ways: in the arc of a game from the stands or a season from the box scores, in photos, or even in numbers. At Baseball Prospectus, we understand that statistics don't replace observation or any of baseball's stories, but complement everything else that makes the game so much fun.

What stats help us with is with patterns and precision, variance and value. This book can help you learn things you may not see from watching a game or hundred, whether it's the path of a career over time or the breadth of the entire MLB. We'd also never ask you to choose between our numbers and the experience of viewing a game from the cheap seats or the comfort of your home; our publication combines running the numbers with observations and wisdom from some of the brightest minds we can find. But if you *do* want to learn more about the numbers beyond what's on the backs of player jerseys, let us help explain.

Offense

At the end of this past year, we've revised our methodology for determining batting value. Long-time readers of Baseball Prospectus will notice that we've retired True Average in favor of a new metric: Deserved Runs Created Plus (DRC+). Developed by Jonathan Judge and our stats team, this statistic measures everything a player does at the plate–reaching base, hitting for power, making outs, and moving runners over–and puts it on a scale where 100 equals league-average performance. A DRC+ of 150 is terrific, a DRC+ of 100 is average, and a DRC+ of 75 means you better be an excellent defender.

DRC+ also does a better job than any of our previous metrics in taking contextual factors into account. The model adjusts for how the park affects performance, but also for things like the talent of the opposing pitcher, value of different types of batted-ball events, league, temperature, and other factors. It's able to describe a player's expected offensive contribution than any other statistic we've found over the years, and also does a better job of predicting future performance as well.

The other aspect of run-scoring is baserunning, which we quantify using Baserunning Runs. BRR not only records the value of stolen bases (or getting caught in the act), but also accounts for a runner's ability to go first to third on a single or advance on a fly ball.

Defense

Where offensive value is *relatively* easy to identify and understand, defensive value is ... not. Over the past dozen years, the sabermetric community has focused mostly on stats based on zone data: a real-live human person records the type of batted ball and estimated landing location, and models are created that give expected outs. From there, you can compare fielders' actual outs to those expected ones. Simple, right?

Unfortunately, zone data has two major issues. First, zone data is recorded by commercial data providers who keep the raw data private unless you pay for it. (All the statistics we build in this book and on our website use public data as inputs.) That hurts our ability to test assumptions or duplicate results. Second, over the years it has become apparent that there's quite a bit of "noise" in zone-based fielding analysis. Sometimes the conclusions drawn from zone data don't hold up to scrutiny, and sometimes the different data provided by different providers don't look anything alike, giving wildly different results. Sometimes the hard-working professional stringers or scorers might unknowingly inflict unconscious bias into the mix: for example good fielders will often be credited with more expected outs despite the data, and ballparks with high press boxes tend to score more line drives than ones with a lower press box.

Enter our Fielding Runs Above Average (FRAA). For most positions, FRAA is built from play-by-play data, which allows us to avoid the subjectivity found in many other fielding metrics. The idea is this: count how many fielding plays are made by a given player and compare that to expected plays for an average fielder at their position (based on pitcher ground-ball tendencies and batter handedness). Then we adjust for park and base-out situations.

When it comes to catchers, our methodology is a little different thanks to the laundry list of responsibilities they're tasked with beyond just, well, catching and throwing the ball. By now you've probably heard about "framing" or the art of making umpires more likely to call balls outside the strike zone for strikes. To put this into one tidy number, we incorporate pitch tracking data (for the years it exists) and adjust for important factors like pitcher, umpire, batter, and home-field advantage using a mixed-model approach. This grants us a number for how many strikes the catcher is personally adding to (or subtracting from) his pitchers' performance ... which we then convert to runs added or lost using linear weights.

Framing is one of the biggest parts of determining catcher value, but we also take into account blocking balls from going past, whether a scorer deems it a passed ball or a wild pitch. We use a similar approach–one that really benefits from the pitch tracking data that tells us what ends up in the dirt and what doesn't. We also include a catcher's ability to prevent stolen bases and how well they field balls in play, and *finally* we come up with our FRAA for catchers.

Pitching

Both pitching and fielding make up the half of baseball that isn't run scoring: run prevention. Separating pitching from fielding is a tough task, and most recent pitching analysis has branched off from Voros McCracken's famous (and controversial) statement, "There is little if any difference among major-league pitchers in their ability to prevent hits on balls hit in the field of play." The research of the analytic community has validated this to some extent, and there are a host of "defense-independent" pitching measures that have been developed to try and extricate the effect of the defense behind a hurler from the pitcher's work.

Our solution to this quandry is Deserved Run Average (DRA), our core pitching metric. DRA looks like earned run average (ERA), the tried-and-true pitching stat you've seen on every baseball broadcast or box score from the past century, but it's very different. To start, DRA takes an event-by-event look at what the pitchers does, and adjusts the value of that event based on different environmental factors like park, batter, catcher, umpire, base-out situation, run differential, inning, defense, home field advantage, pitcher role, and temperature. That mixed model gives us a pitcher's expected contribution, similar to what we do for our DRC+ model for hitters and FRAA model for catchers. (Oh, and we also consider the pitcher's effect on basestealing and on balls getting past the catcher.)

It's important to note that DRA is set to the scale of runs allowed per nine innings (RA9) instead of ERA, which makes DRA's scale slightly higher than ERA's. The reason for this is because ERA tends to overrate three types of pitchers:

1. Pitchers who play in parks where scorers hand out more errors. Official scorers differ significantly in the frequency at which they assign errors to fielders.
2. Ground-ball pitchers, because a substantial proportion of errors occur on grounders.
3. Pitchers who aren't very good. Better pitchers often allow fewer unearned runs than bad pitchers, because good pitchers tend to find ways to get out of jams.

Since the last time you picked up an edition of this book, we've also made a few minor changes to DRA to make it better. Recent research into "tunneling"–the act of throwing consecutive pitches that appear similar from a batter's point of view until after the swing decision point–data has given us a new contextual factor to account for in DRA: plate distance. This refers to the distance between successive pitches as they approach the plate, and while it has a smaller effect than factors like velocity or whiff rate, it still can help explain pitcher strikeout rate in our model.

New Pitching Metrics for 2019

We're including a few "new" pitching metrics for 2019's suite of Baseball Prospectus publications, but you may be familiar with them if you've spent time scouring the internet for stats.

Fastball Percentage

Our fastball percentage (FB%) statistic measures how frequently a pitcher throws a pitch classified as a "fastball," measured as a percentage of overall pitches thrown. We qualify three types of fastballs:

1. The traditional four-seam fastball;
2. The two-seam fastball or sinker;
3. "Hard cutters," which are pitches that have the movement profile of a cut fastball and are used as the pitcher's primary offering or in place of a more traditional fastball.

For example, a pitcher with a FB% of 67 throws any combination of these three pitches about two-thirds of the time.

Whiff Rate

Everybody loves a swing and a miss, and whiff rate (WHF) measures how frequently pitchers induce a swinging strike. To calculate WHF, we add up all the pitches thrown that ended with a swinging strike, then divide that number by a pitcher's total pitches thrown. Most often, high whiff rates correlate with high strikeout rates (and overall effective pitcher performance).

Called Strike Probability

Called Strike Probability (CSP) is a number that represents the likelihood that all of a pitcher's pitches will be called a strike while controlling for location, pitcher and batter handedness, umpire and count. Here's how it works: on each pitch, our model determines how many times (out of 100) that a similar pitch was called for a strike given those factors mentioned above, and when normalized for each batter's strike zone. Then we average the CSP for all pitches thrown by a pitcher in a season, and that gives us the yearly CSP percentage you see in the stats boxes.

As you might imagine, pitchers with a higher CSP are more likely to work in the zone, where pitchers with a lower CSP are likely locating their pitches outside the normal strike zone, for better or for worse.

Projections

Many of you aren't turning to this book just for a look at what a player has done, but for a look at what a player is going to do: the PECOTA projections. PECOTA, initially developed by Nate Silver (who has moved on to greater fame as a political analyst), consists of three parts:

1. Major-league equivalencies, which use minor-league statistics to project how a player will perform in the major leagues;
2. Baseline forecasts, which use weighted averages and regression to the mean to estimate a player's current true talent level; and
3. Aging curves, which uses the career paths of comparable players to estimate how a player's statistics are likely to change over time.

With all those important things covered, let's take a look at what's in the book this year.

Team Prospectus

You bought this book to learn more about your favorite (or maybe least-favorite, who are we to judge?) team, so let's talk about them. After a thoughtful preview of the 2019 season, you'll be presented with our Team Prospectus. This outlines many of the key statistics for each team's 2018 season, as well as a very inviting stadium diagram.

First you'll find the Performance Graphs page. The first is the 2018 Hit List Ranking. This shows our Hit List Rank for the team on each day of the 2018 season and is intended to give you a picture of the ups and downs of the team's season, including their highest and lowest ranks of the year. Hit List Rank measures overall team performance and drives the Hit List Power Rankings at the baseballprospectus.com website.

The second graph is Committed Payroll and helps you see how the team's payroll has compared to the MLB and divisional average payrolls over time. Payroll figures are currents as of January 1, 2019; with so many free agents still unsigned as of this writing, the final 2018 figure will likely be significantly different for many teams. (In the meantime, you can always find the most current data at Baseball Prospectus' Cot's Baseball Contracts page.)

Cincinnati Reds 2019

The third graph is Farm System Ranking and displays how the Baseball Prospectus prospect team has ranked the organization's farm system since 2007. It also indicates the highest and lowest ranks that the farm system achieved over that time.

We start the Team Performance page with the squad's unadjusted and third-order 2018 win-loss records, presented in divisional context. We then list the three highest performing hitters and pitchers by WARP for 2018. Beneath that are a host of other team statistics. **Pythag** presents an adjusted 2018 winning percentage, calculated by taking runs scored per game (**RS/G**) and runs allowed per game (**RA/G**) for the team, and running them through a version of Bill James' Pythagorean formula that was refined and improved by David Smyth and Brandon Heipp. (The formula is called "Pythagenpat," which is equally fun to type and to say.)

Next up is **DRC+**, described earlier, to indicate the overall hitting ability of the team either above or below league-average. Run prevention on the pitching side is covered by **DRA** (also mentioned earlier) and another metric: Fielding Independent Pitching (**FIP**), which calculates another ERA-like statistic based on strikeouts, walks, and home runs recorded. Defensive Efficiency Rating (**DER**) tells us the percentage of balls in play turned into outs for the team, and is a quick fielding shorthand that rounds out run prevention.

After that, we have several measures related to roster composition, as opposed to on-field performance. **B-Age** and **P-Age** tell us the average age of a team's batters and pitchers, respectively. **Salary** is the combined team payroll for all on-field players, and Doug Pappas' Marginal Dollars per Marginal Win (**M$/MW**) tells us how much money a team spent to earn production above replacement level.

Ending this batch of statistics is the number of disabled list days a team had over the season (**DL Days**) and the amount of salary paid to players on the disabled list (**$ on DL**); this final number is expressed as a percentage of total payroll.

Next to each of these stats, we've listed each team's MLB rank in that category from 1st to 30th. In this, 1st always indicates a positive outcome and 30th a negative outcome, except in the case of salary–1st is highest.

The Team Projections page is intended to convey the team's operational capacity entering the 2019 season. We start with the team's PECOTA projected record for 2019, again in divisional context. The **+/-** column indicates how many more or less wins the team is projected to get than they got in 2018. We then list the three highest projected hitters and pitchers by WARP for 2018. A brief farm system summary follows, with the team's top prospect and number of BP Top 101 Prospects. Finally, we list the key new players and departed players, along with their 2019 projected WARP.

Alex Bregman 3B

Born: 03/30/94 Age: 25 Bats: R Throws: R
Height: 6'0" Weight: 180 Origin: Round 1, 2015 Draft (#2 overall)

YEAR	TEAM	LVL	AGE	PA	R	2B	3B	HR	RBI	BB	K	SB	CS	AVG/OBP/SLG
2016	CCH	AA	22	285	54	16	2	14	46	42	26	5	3	.297/.415/.559
2016	FRE	AAA	22	83	17	6	0	6	15	5	12	2	1	.333/.373/.641
2016	HOU	MLB	22	217	31	13	3	8	34	15	52	2	0	.264/.313/.478
2017	HOU	MLB	23	626	88	39	5	19	71	55	97	17	5	.284/.352/.475
2018	HOU	MLB	24	705	105	51	1	31	103	96	85	10	4	.286/.394/.532
2019	HOU	MLB	25	675	96	38	3	23	78	73	107	12	4	.272/.359/.463

Breakout: 6% Improve: 52% Collapse: 5% Attrition: 2% MLB: 100%
Comparables: Anthony Rendon, David Wright, Pablo Sandoval

YEAR	TEAM	LVL	AGE	PA	DRC+	VORP	BABIP	BRR	FRAA	WARP
2016	CCH	AA	22	285	172	38.9	.286	1.6	SS(51): -3.4, 3B(11): 1.4	2.7
2016	FRE	AAA	22	83	161	10.0	.333	-1.2	SS(14): 2.1, LF(3): -0.1	0.8
2016	HOU	MLB	22	217	107	9.6	.317	0.5	3B(40): 0.9, SS(6): -0.1	1.1
2017	HOU	MLB	23	626	114	34.7	.311	-1.5	3B(132): 8.7, SS(30): -2.9	3.9
2018	HOU	MLB	24	705	150	72.6	.289	-1.6	3B(136): 5.4, SS(28): -0.4	7.4
2019	HOU	MLB	25	675	125	37.3	.295	0.0	3B 7, SS 0	4.6

After the projections page, we share a few items about the team's home ballpark. There's the aforementioned diagram of the park's dimensions (including distances to the outfield wall), a few important biographical facts about the stadium, a graphic showing the height of the wall from the left-field pole to the right-field pole, and a table showing three-year park factors for the stadium. The park factors are displayed as indexes where 100 is average, 110 means that the park inflates the statistic in question by 10 percent, and 90 means that the park deflates the statistic in question by 10 percent.

Following the ballpark page, we have a **Personnel** section that lists many of the important decision-makers and upper-level field and operations staff members for the franchise, as well as any former Baseball Prospectus staff members who are currently part of the organization.

Position Players

After all that information and a thoughtful bylined essay covering each team, we present our player comments. Each player is listed with the major-league team who employed him as of early January 2019. If a player changed teams after that point via free agency, trade, or any other method, you'll be able to find them in the book for their previous squad.

First, we cover biographical information (age is as of June 30, 2019) before moving onto the stats themselves. Our statistic columns include standard identifying information like **YEAR**, **TEAM**, **LVL** (level of affiliated play) and **AGE** before getting into the numbers. Next, we provide raw, unstranslated numbers like you might find on the back of your dad's baseball cards: **PA** (plate appearances), **R** (runs), **2B** (doubles), **3B** (triples), **HR** (home runs), **RBI** (runs batted in), **BB** (walks), **K** (strikeouts), **SB** (stolen bases) and **CS** (caught stealing). Then we have unadjusted "slash" statistics: **AVG** (batting average), **OBP** (on-base percentage) and **SLG** (slugging percentage).

Just below the stats box is **PECOTA** data, which is discussed further in a following section. After that, it's on to a pithy and always-informative comment written by a member of the Baseball Prospectus staff, before we cover more stats.

The second text box repeats YEAR, TEAM, LVL, AGE, and PA, then moves on to **DRC+** (Deserved Runs Created Plus), which we described earlier as total offensive expected contribution compared to the league average. Next, one of our oldest active metrics, **VORP** (Value Over Replacement Player), considers offensive production, position and plate appearances. In essence, it is the number of runs contributed beyond what a replacement-level player at the same position would contribute if given the same percentage of team plate appearances. VORP does not consider the quality of a player's defense.

BABIP (batting average on balls in play) tells us how often a ball in play fell for a hit, and can help us identify whether a batter may have been lucky or not … but note that high BABIPs also tend to follow the great hitters of our time, as well as speedy singles hitters who put the ball on the ground.

The next item is **BRR** (Baserunning Runs), which covers all of a player's baserunning accomplishments which includes (but isn't limited to) swiped bags and failed attempts. Next is **FRAA** (Fielding Runs Above Average), which also includes the number of games previously played at each position noted in parentheses. Multi-position players have only their two most frequent positions listed here, but their total FRAA number reflects all positions played.

Our last column here is **WARP** (Wins Above Replacement Player). WARP estimates the total value of a player, which means for hitters it takes into account hitting runs above average (calculated using the DRC+ model), BRR and FRAA. Then, it makes an adjustment for positions played and gives the player a credit for plate appearances based upon the difference between "replacement level"¬–which is derived from the quality of players added to a team's roster after the start of the season¬–and the league average.

Catchers

Catchers are a special breed, and thus they have earned their own separate box which displays some of the defensive metrics that we've built just for them. As an example, let's check out J.T. Realmuto.

YEAR	TEAM	P. COUNT	FRM RUNS	BLK RUNS	THRW RUNS	TOT RUNS
2016	MIA	18935	-8.5	1.8	2.1	-5.6
2017	MIA	18959	5.3	1.7	1.0	9.1
2018	MIA	16399	-0.4	0.9	0.1	0.4
2019	PHI	18448	-1.4	1.5	0.7	0.8

The **YEAR** and **TEAM** columns match what you'd find in the other stat box. **P. COUNT** indicates the number of pitches thrown while the catcher was behind the plate, including swinging strikes, fouls, and balls in play. **FRM RUNS** is the total run value the catcher provided (or cost) his team by influencing the umpire to call strikes where other catchers did not. **BLK RUNS** expresses the total run value above or below average for the catcher's ability to prevent wild pitches and passed balls. **THRW RUNS** is calculated using a similar model as the previous two statistics, and it measures a catcher's ability to throw out basestealers but also to dissuade them from testing his arm in the first place. It takes into account factors like the pitcher (including his delivery and pickoff move) and baserunner (who could be as fast as Billy Hamilton or as slow as Yonder Alonso). **TOT RUNS** is the sum of all of the previous three statistics.

Pitchers

Let's give our pitchers a turn, using 2018 NL Cy Young winner Jacob deGrom as our example. Take a look at his first stat block: the first line and the **YEAR**, **TEAM**, **LVL** and **AGE** columns are the same as in the position player example earlier.

Here too, we have a series of columns that display raw, unadjusted statistics compiled by the pitcher over the course of a season: **W** (wins), **L** (losses), **SV** (saves), **G** (games pitched), **GS** (games started), **IP** (innings pitched), **H** (hits allowed) and **HR** (home runs allowed). Next we have two statistics that are rates: **BB/9** (walks per nine innings) and **K/9** (strikeouts per nine innings), before returning to the unadjusted **K** (strikeouts).

Next up is **GB%** (ground ball percentage), which is the percentage of all batted balls that were hit in the ground, including both outs and hits. Remember, this is based on observational data and subject to human error, so please approach this with a healthy dose of skepticism.

BABIP (batting average on balls in play) is calculated using the same methodology as it is for position players, but it often tells us more about a pitcher than it does a hitter. With pitchers, a high BABIP is often due to poor defense or bad luck, and can often be an indicator of potential rebound, and a low BABIP may be cause to expect performance regression. (A typical league-average BABIP is close to .290-.300.)

After a witty 150ish words on the player like only Baseball Prospectus's staff can provide, it's on to that second stat block, which repeats the YEAR, TEAM, LVL, and AGE columns. The metrics **WHIP** (walks plus hits per inning pitched) and **ERA** (earned run average) are old standbys: WHIP measures walks and hits allowed on a per-inning basis, while ERA measures earned runs on a nine-inning basis. Neither of these stats are translated or adjusted.

DRA (Deserved Run Average) was described at length earlier, and measures how many runs the pitcher "deserved" to allow per nine innings. Please note that since we lack all the data points that would make for a "real" DRA for minor-league events, the DRA displayed for minor league partial-seasons is based off of different data. (That data is a modified version of our cFIP metric, which you can find more information about on our website.)

Jacob deGrom   RHP
Born: 06/19/88   Age: 31   Bats: L   Throws: R
Height: 6'4"   Weight: 180   Origin: Round 9, 2010 Draft (#272 overall)

YEAR	TEAM	LVL	AGE	W	L	SV	G	GS	IP	H	HR	BB/9	K/9	K	GB%	BABIP
2016	NYN	MLB	28	7	8	0	24	24	148	142	15	2.2	8.7	143	47%	.312
2017	NYN	MLB	29	15	10	0	31	31	201[1]	180	28	2.6	10.7	239	48%	.305
2018	NYN	MLB	30	10	9	0	32	32	217	152	10	1.9	11.2	269	48%	.281
2019	NYN	MLB	31	13	9	0	31	31	186	145	18	2.3	10.7	221	46%	.286

Breakout: 8%   Improve: 29%   Collapse: 28%   Attrition: 6%   MLB: 85%
Comparables: Erik Bedard, A.J. Burnett, CC Sabathia

YEAR	TEAM	LVL	AGE	WHIP	ERA	DRA	WARP	MPH	FB%	WHF	CSP
2016	NYN	MLB	28	1.20	3.04	3.30	3.5	96.3	59.6	12.1	47.2
2017	NYN	MLB	29	1.19	3.53	3.02	5.7	97.2	55.5	14.5	49.5
2018	NYN	MLB	30	0.91	1.70	2.09	8.0	98.2	52.1	16.3	48.4
2019	NYN	MLB	31	1.02	2.91	3.23	3.9	96.6	54.5	14.8	48.2

Just like with hitters, **WARP** (Wins Above Replacement Player) is a total value metric that puts pitchers of all stripes on the same scale as position players. We use DRA as the primary input for our calculation of WARP. You might notice that relief pitchers (due to their limited innings) may have a lower WARP than you were expecting or than you might see in other WARP-like metrics. WARP does not take leverage into account, just the actions a pitcher performs and the expected value of those actions … which ends up judging high-leverage relief pitchers differently than you might imagine given their prestige and market value.

MPH gives you the pitcher's 95th percentile velocity for the noted season, in order to give you an idea of what the *peak* fastball velocity a pitcher possesses. Since this comes from our pitch tracking data, it is not publicly available for minor-league pitchers.

Finally, we display the three new pitching metrics we described earlier. **FB%** (fastball percentage) gives you the percentage of fastballs thrown out of all pitches. **WhiffRt** (whiff rate) tells you the percentage of swinging strikes induced out of all pitches. **CS Prob** (called strike probability) expresses the likelihood of all pitches thrown to result in a called strike, after controlling for factors like handedness, umpire, pitch type, count, and location.

PECOTA

All players have PECOTA projections for 2019, as well as a set of other numbers that describe the performance of comparable players according to PECOTA. All projections for 2019 are for the player at the date we went to press in early January and are projected into the league and park context as indicated by the team abbreviation. All PECOTA projected statistics represent a player's projected major-league performance.

The numbers beneath the player's stats–Breakout, Improve, Collapse, Attrition–are part and parcel of the PECOTA projections. They estimate the likelihood of changes in performance relative to the player's previously-established level of production, based on the performance of comparable players:

Breakout Rate is the percent change that a player's production will improve by at least 20 percent relative to the weighted average of his performance over his most recent seasons.

Improve Rate is the percent chance that a player's production will improve at all relative to his baseline performance. A player who is expected to perform just the same as he has in the recent past will have an Improve Rate of 50 percent.

Collapse Rate is the percent chance that a position player's production will decline by at least 25 percent relative to his baseline performance.

Attrition Rate operates on playing time rather than performance. Specifically, it measures the likelihood that a player's playing time will decrease by at least 50 percent relative to his established level.

Breakout Rate and Collapse Rate can sometimes be counterintuitive for players who have already experienced a radical change in performance level. It's also worth noting that the projected decline in a player's rate performances might not be indicative of an expected decline in underlying ability or skill, but could just be an anticipated correction following a breakout season.

MLB% is the percentage of similar players who played in the major leagues in their relevant season.

The final pieces of information are the player's three highest-scoring comparable players as determined by PECOTA. All comparables represent a snapshot of how the listed player was performing at the same age as the current player, so if a 23-year-old pitcher is compared to Bartolo Colon, he's actually being compared to a 23-year-old Colon, not the version that pitched for the Rangers in 2018, nor to Colon's career as a whole.

Cincinnati Reds 2019

A few points about pitcher projections. First, we aren't yet projecting peak velocity, so that column will be blank in the PECOTA lines. Second, projecting DRA is trickier than evaluating past performance, because it is unclear how deserving each pitcher will be of his anticipated outcomes. However, we know that another DRA-related statistic–contextual FIP or cFIP–estimates future run scoring very well. So for PECOTA, the projected DRA figures you see are based on the past cFIPs generated by the pitcher and comparable players over time, along with the other factors described above.

Lineouts

In each chapter's Lineouts section, you'll find abbreviated text comments, as well as most of same information you'd find in our full player comments. We limit the stats boxes in this section to only including the 2018 information for each player.

Exclusive Player Visualizations

In our constant battle to provide you with new and interesting baseball content you can't find anywhere else, we've added a trio of data visualizations to each hitter's entry in these books and a pair of visualizations for each pitcher.

For hitters, you'll find three new infographics. The first is each player's **Batted Ball Distribution**, which displays the five major sections of the field: LF (left), LCF (left center), CF (center), RCF (right center), and RF (right). The percentage indicated tells us what percentage of batted balls from that hitter fell within that part of the field during the 2018 season. We've also included the hitter's slugging percentage on balls in play (also called **SLGCON**) for that part of the field.

You'll also see two heatmaps: **Strike Zone vs LHP** and **Strike Zone vs RHP**. These heat maps represent a view of the strike zone from behind the catcher. Areas where there is a darker coloration represent the places where a higher percentage of pitches resulted in hits. In other words, the heatmap represents a hitter's "sweet spots" for getting hits against either left-handed or right-handed pitchers, depending on the image.

Pitchers get two images that help explain what their pitches look like from a hitter's perspective: **Pitch Shape vs LHH** and **Pitch Shape vs RHH**. These images show you the shape and the "tunneling" effect of each pitcher's offerings from the batter's perspective. For each type of pitch that a pitcher throws (represented by an indicator shape), there's a set of dots indicating the flight path, where each dot represents a 0.01-second interval. This maps the average trajectory and speed of an offering, ending where the ball crosses the plate. The solid black box represents the regular strike zone, while the gray contour lines indicate the range of locations that a pitcher typically works in.

Below the image, we provide a bit more detailed information about each pitcher's average offering in the **Pitch Types** box. Here, we also list each of the pitcher's major offerings under the **Type** column.

- **Fastballs** (which usually refers to the four-seam variation)
- **Sinkers** and/or two-seam fastballs
- **Cutters** (which could include "hard" cutters like cut fastballs and "soft" cutters that resemble hard sliders)
- **Changeups** (not including most splitters)
- **Splitters** (split-fingered pitches, forkballs, and some split-changes)
- **Sliders** and/or slurves
- **Curveballs** (including spike-curveballs and knuckle-curveballs, as well as some slurvy curves)
- **Slow curveballs** and/or eephus pitches
- **Knuckleballs**
- **Screwballs**

The **Freq** column indicates the percentage of overall pitches that fall into each of those type categories; if a pitcher has a 16.55% score for changeups, then that's the percent of all pitches that he throws as changeups. **Velo** is exactly what you think it is: the average miles per hour for each pitch type. **H Mov** is the number of inches of horizontal movement on the average pitch of that type, while **V Mov** is the number of inches of vertical movement on the average pitch of that type. (At Baseball Prospectus, we measure this over the long flight of the ball and include gravity into the V Mov number in order to give you the most realistic representation of what the pitch *actually* does.)

If you're wondering about the second number in brackets, that's the index for that velocity or movement compared to the league average. Like DRC+, a score of 100 means that the speed or movement is about the same as league average, while a higher score means that there's higher velocity or movement than the league average. Numbers below 100 indicate less velocity or movement than the league average.

Part 1: Team Analysis

Table for Two: Previewing the 2019 Cincinnati Reds

Roger Cormier and Nicholas Zettel

ROGER CORMIER: The 2019 Reds are definitely a 2001 Jimmy Eat World song. "A Praise Chorus" perhaps. They could have easily slept through the offseason, gestured vaguely towards the rest of the NL Central to their fans and rhetorically asked "What do you expect us to do, exactly?", sold a decent number of tickets and buzz for the 150th anniversary of the Cincinnati Red Stockings and The Joey Votto Experience (which comedy personality will he talk to next?!) and call it a honorable day by contemporary MLB standards. But the Reds tried! To a point. "Sweetness!" an Arizona based-band might say.

Yasiel Puig, Matt Kemp, Sonny Gray, Alex Wood, Tanner Roark, and Zach Duke are all definitely major league baseball players. Puig and Votto on the same team is a particular visual I preemptively am enjoying (name a more ambitious crossover.) They pried Dodgers hitting coach Turner Ward and Brewers pitching coach Derek Johnson away from their respective really good squads.

Then I look at the meh $143.2 million luxury tax payroll, and at the PECOTA projections, and get the feeling the front office wanted to just put up some slightly fancier wallpaper in a drafty apartment. The Reds, incredibly enough, are projected to lead the National League in runs scored. Also in runs allowed. And those numbers are one in the same: 755. So their aim was a sneaky Hank Aaron tribute? Or maybe it was to finish 81-81, tied for third in a five-team division. I can't think of a Jimmy Eat World song title for this scenario, sadly. Can you, Nicholas?

NICHOLAS ZETTEL: Like the bulk of the 2019 National League, the Reds are certainly in the middle. I think "the Reds tried" narrative has gained so much steam throughout the offseason because they reminded baseball fans that it's fun to watch teams attempt to improve their rosters, and their moves largely fly in the face of MLB's recent "tank", er, "rebuild for the future" logic. Compared to a Polar Vortex offseason, even windbreaker weather feels nice.

In the current MLB environment, I can see how some people would view the Reds' offseason as a failure: if a team is stuck in a tough division with a few contending teams, if a team is about to graduate a prospect like Nick Senzel, if a team has *only* produced five consecutive losing seasons, what good is a season in which they might win 81 games and maybe contend for a Wild Card if things go right? There's certainly a contingency of baseball fans who believed the Reds should just be bad and take the chance at increased draft bonus money in 2019. But this script can also be flipped: if you're going to be graduating top prospects, and one of the game's behemoth markets wants to shed talent like Kemp, Puig, and Wood to reduce their luxury tax burden, why not pounce on those extra wins?

ROGER: The Reds are right there with you, saying yes to that rhetorical question. They also uniquely enough replaced 60 percent of their starting rotation.

NICHOLAS: That helps—heading into the offseason, the Reds sure didn't have a pitching staff that matched contending expectations. Their starters with the heaviest workloads boasted rather high Deserved Run Average (DRA): Luis Castillo (4.76), Sal Romano (5.76), Matt Harvey (4.79), Tyler Mahle (6.30), and Anthony DeSclafani (5.16) started 124 games in 2018. Even if Cincinnati returned this same starting group, it wouldn't be faulty to say there's nowhere to go but up.

But analysts no longer require wishful thinking to imagine decent Reds pitching. PECOTA projects Castillo (3.89 DRA), Tanner Roark (4.59), DeSclafani (5.00), Sonny Gray (4.09), and Alex Wood (3.86) to start 116 games in 2019. It's fun to dream on a team winning more games when a young talent like Castillo takes a step forward, but even a solid rotational depth arm like Roark improves the team just by showing up.

ROGER: Oh, Tanner Roark might kill one of his fielders. PECOTA believes the Reds will end up with the second worst defense (-15.4 FRAA) in the National League this year, only bettering the Phillies, an organization I am almost certain has internal debates over the correct pronunciation of "defense". I get why they ditched Billy Hamilton (the whole "offense" thing); the thing is they did not replace him with an actual center fielder. Top prospect Nick Senzel is going to try even though he only played infield in the minor leagues and underwent two surgeries last season (and suffered for a stretch with vertigo). Scott Schebler is set for 224 plate appearances as a center fielder in 2019, exactly one better than Senzel in the middle (*applause*). He currently has 177 PAs as a center fielder throughout his career. His sprint speed last season ranked 210th out of 549 players (Billy Hamilton tied for 4th). He tied George Springer, so at least it won't be a disaster. And I read Michael Lorenzen is working in the outfield this spring...

NICHOLAS: ... I can see it now, the Reds clinching the NL Central with Lorenzen credited as the pitcher of record after hitting a homer and catching the final fly out....

ROGER: Your move, Ohtani.

NICHOLAS: I think it's also worth questioning the potential impact of Derek Johnson as pitching coach. Typically, it's difficult to quantify the actual production of a pitching coach, but Johnson's trick in Milwaukee was largely to help a group of pitchers with notable scouting flaws "play up" to their strengths, implement long-term mechanical improvements, and hone in on certain pitches for development. It didn't work for everyone, but it worked enough to win. He's also got the zen side of coaching down, with the process-oriented "be great at what you're good at" Yogi Berra-ism. Without entering the realm of magical thinking about a coach's role, I can't help but see some parallels between an underwhelming Reds staff working within a difficult ballpark and the surprising pitching staff of the 2018 Brewers.

ROGER: Derek was Sonny Gray's pitching coach at Vanderbilt, and this reunion could be called the Old Gray Whisperer Test if you don't mind losing all of your friends.

I'm curious about the team using Raisel Iglesias in high-leverage situations instead of in the traditional closer's role. Iglesias says he's cool with it, which is a key first step to implementing such a plan. There's a good chance though it simply won't last for very long if at all due to a lack of comfort from Raisel and a finite amount of patience from the rest of the bullpen. PECOTA sees a regression with Iglesias, dropping from a 1.2 WARP last season to 0.7, which is in line with Statcast saying he was more lucky than not in 2018. PECOTA also thinks he will throw 18 fewer innings than last season, so shrug emoji.

NICHOLAS: The old saying applies here: "Iglesias, Duke and Hughes and pray for rain and maybe a new outfield fence configuration or a humidor." Good thing these Reds will R-A-K-E. That's how they're going to compete, right?

ROGER: Scooter Gennett, Jose Peraza, and Eugenio Suarez are not going to repeat their really good to great 2018 work, and that's just fine. They are going to be really healthy in September not having to carry an entire team on their shoulders. Puig (2.5 projected WARP), a healthy Jesse Winker (1.5), Tucker Barnhart (1.0), Scott Schebler (2.1), and that Votto guy (5.1) are all set to improve upon last year and pick up the boom stick slack.

NICHOLAS: I don't think that the season will be doomed for the Reds even if they don't contend, which makes 2019 a bizarre kind of win-win. Imagine a scenario where the club plays well early on, maybe faltering under the weight of the midseason crunch. Guys like Iglesias, Puig, Wood, or even Jared Hughes, Gennett, and Roark could be reasonable trade deadline fodder. If you're a contending MLB exec at the deadline, would you trade prospects for these guys?

ROGER: If the hitters succeed on the road before the deadline, and if the hurlers save their worst appearances for Great American Ball Park, absolutely. A potential nightmare though is if it's July 28 and Cincinnati is something like four games behind first place with three teams ahead of them in the division. Fans will be screaming at one another in between bites of Skyline Chili over whether or not their team should bail, add, or stay put. At least it'll be interesting.

NICHOLAS: This just seems like the front office pulled off the best possible gamble. Even in "failure" the club could make a quick reboot of the system, develop some prospects at the MLB level, and have less than $60 million in guaranteed payroll heading into the offseason. Rob Manfred just whispered, "Pinch me, I'm dreaming," into my ear.

ROGER: Rob needs to learn some boundaries. Speaking of, who is gonna break out (of their metaphysical boxes)?

NICHOLAS: I'd say we call Joey Votto and Yasiel Puig the co-breakout and hit lunch. But PECOTA really likes CF Nick Senzel, Luis Castillo, Sonny Gray, Tyler Mahle, Michael Lorenzen… and Scott Schebler!

ROGER: I'm worried about Senzel's injuries. Gray gets to escape Yankee Stadium where he was pretty damn bad. Unfortunately, his new home office is the equally offensive Great American Ballpark. Mahle is technically going to have the biggest improvement this year according to PECOTA (from -1.3 WARP to 0.7), and Votto and Schebler are tied for the second biggest (1.4 WARP increases).

NICHOLAS: The Reds drafted Tyler Mahle in the 7th round in 2013 and he ranked fifth on the 2018 Reds Top Ten as a quintessential mid-rotation arm. So a 95 IP, 18 start, 4.41 DRA projection feels like someone taught PECOTA how to read scouting reports.

ROGER: Let's say it was me.

NICHOLAS: So you must know that Joey Votto is a true benefactor of the under-the-hood tweaks that made PECOTA more aggressive. What do you think about the Reds first base anchor?

ROGER: Votto turns 36 in September, but he'll be a *Canadian* 36.

Okay, I have been told a Canadian 36 is the same as an American 36, so his WARP decline from 6.5 in 2017 to 3.8 in 2018 could have to do with age. It also has to do with his name—Joey Bat Control in his "down" season still came away with the third best on-base percentage in the game. Besides, Statcast thinks some of his decline had to do with bad breaks: Votto finished with the 34th least lucky difference between wOBA (.370) and xwOBA (.390) last season among the 313 batters with over 250 plate appearances, and he was the 18th least fortuitous when it came to SLG (.419) and xSLG (.472).

PECOTA thinks the full-season career-low 12 home runs he clubbed in 2018 are more of an anomaly than anything and it will improve to 20 to go along with a 5.1 WARP. 20 home runs looks a lot better coming from a mid-30s first baseman than 12. It is only four home runs fewer than division rival Anthony Rizzo is expected to mash, and five fewer than Cardinals newbie Paul Goldschmidt. Votto's anticipated .499 SLG beats those two young whippersnappers, in fact.

So Votto should be fine. PECOTA thinks Schebler is going to get plenty of playing time in the seemingly crowded outfield and go up from a 0.7 to 2.1 WARP despite similar looking slash lines, so he is someone to keep more than a weather eye on. Matt Bowman could be a sneaky good waiver pickup by the team. PECOTA likes Sal Romano with a significant decrease in workload. But neither are Joseph Votto.

Now that we know everything, what do you think their record will actually be?

NICHOLAS: My gut says 85 but the Brewers, Cardinals, and Cubs say 77. I think this is exactly the blend of young players and supplemental talent that could leap from the cellar to make some contending noise. It's also exactly the blend of young players and supplemental talent that could fade from contention during the dog days.

ROGER: Provided the Reds just try their best, and try everything they can, and not worry with what we tell ourselves while they're away playing the actual games, I can kind of see them competing for a division title with the Brewers no longer possessing their out-getter magic. However, I ultimately envision an 82-80 campaign. An entertaining 82-80, but an 82-80 year all the same.

Performance Graphs

2018 Hit List Ranking

Committed Payroll (in millions)

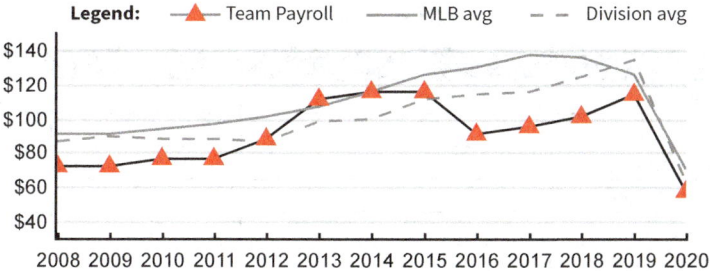

Farm System Ranking

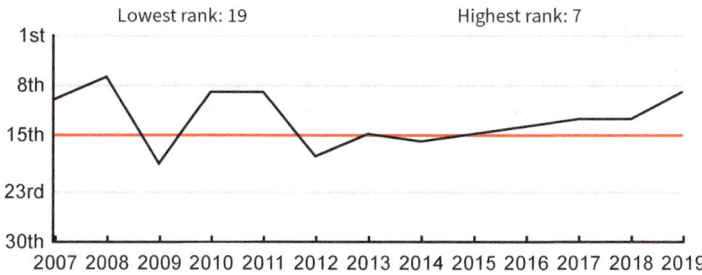

2018 Team Performance

ACTUAL STANDINGS

Team	W	L	Pct
MIL	96	67	.588
CHN	95	68	.582
SLN	88	74	.543
PIT	82	79	.509
CIN	**67**	**95**	**.413**

THIRD-ORDER STANDINGS

Team	W	L	Pct
MIL	93	70	.570
CHN	92	71	.564
SLN	83	79	.512
PIT	78	83	.484
CIN	**71**	**91**	**.438**

TOP HITTERS

Player	WARP
Eugenio Suarez	3.8
Joey Votto	3.7
Jose Peraza	3.1

TOP PITCHERS

Player	WARP
Raisel Iglesias	1.2
Luis Castillo	1.1
Tanner Rainey	1

VITAL STATISTICS

Statistic Name	Value	Rank
Pythagenpat	.423	24th
Runs Scored per Game	4.30	18th
Runs Allowed per Game	5.06	25th
Deserved Runs Created Plus	94	19th
Deserved Run Average	5.34	26th
Fielding Independent Pitching	4.62	25th
Defensive Efficiency Rating	.700	22nd
Batter Age	27.2	6th
Pitcher Age	26.9	5th
Salary	$101.3M	22nd
Marginal $ per Marginal Win	$4.8M	11th
Disabled List Days	$651.0M	1st
$ on DL	9%	4th

2019 Team Projections

PROJECTED STANDINGS

Team	W	L	Pct	+/-
MIL	88	74	.543	-8
SLN	85	77	.524	-3
CIN	**81**	**81**	**.500**	**+14**
PIT	80	82	.493	-2
CHN	79	83	.487	-16

TOP PROJECTED HITTERS

Player	WARP
Joey Votto	5.1
Yasiel Puig	2.4
Eugenio Suarez	2.3

TOP PROJECTED PITCHERS

Player	WARP
Luis Castillo	2.2
Sonny Gray	1.4
Alex Wood	1.4

FARM SYSTEM REPORT

Top Prospect	Number of Top 101 Prospects
Nick Senzel, #9	4

KEY DEDUCTIONS

Player	WARP
Billy Hamilton	0.9
Matt Harvey	0.7

KEY ADDITIONS

Player	WARP
Yasiel Puig	2.4
Sonny Gray	1.4
Alex Wood	1.4
Jose Iglesias	1.4
Derek Dietrich	1.2
Tanner Roark	0.8
Matt Kemp	0.7

Team Personnel

Executive Advisor to the CEO
Walt Jocketty

President, Baseball Operations
Dick Williams

VP, General Manager
Nick Krall

VP, Assistant General Manager
Sam Grossman

Manager
David Bell

BP Alumni
Stuart Wallace

Great American Ball Park Stats

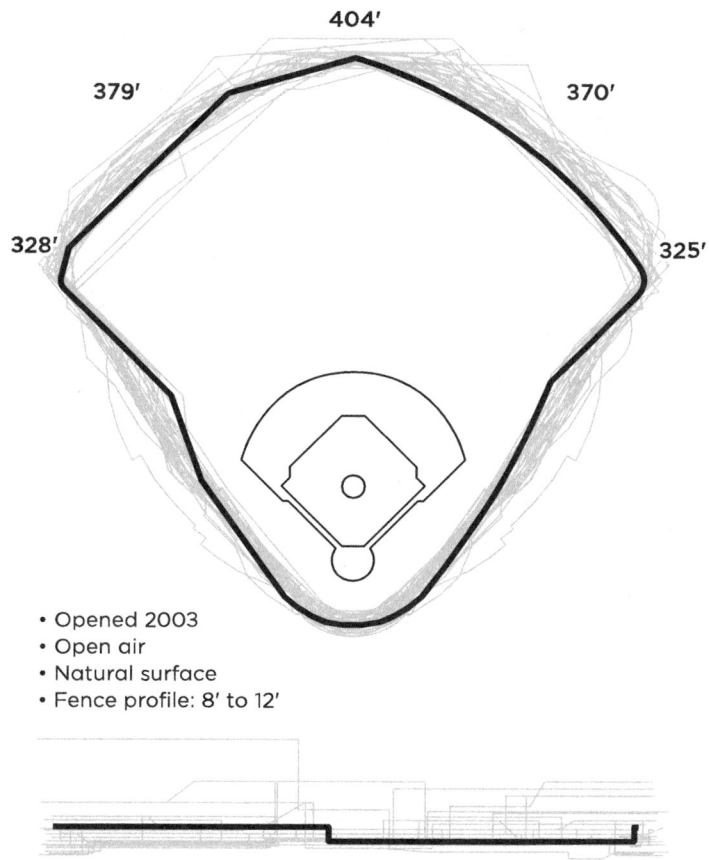

- Opened 2003
- Open air
- Natural surface
- Fence profile: 8' to 12'

Three-Year Park Factors

Runs	Runs/RH	Runs/LH	HR/RH	HR/LH
101	99	104	110	111

Reds Team Analysis

What exactly are they selling at Great American Ball Park these days? It sure isn't winning baseball. The Reds concluded 2018 with their fourth-straight last-place finish and 90-loss season. Cincinnati area baseball fans have responded as you would expect. Attendance fell to 1.6 million in 2018, the lowest mark not only in the Great American Ball Park era (since 2000), but the city's lowest mark since 1984.

Since the move to the new park, the Reds have made just three playoff appearances and won just two playoff games—none of which were won in their home city. The 2012 team was certainly the pinnacle of the Joey Votto Reds squads, a club that won 97 games and looked primed to make a run to the World Series after beating the San Francisco Giants twice at AT&T Park to open the NLDS. Instead, the Reds offense laid an egg in the two subsequent home games as they scored just four combined runs and allowed the series to return to San Francisco for a decisive Game 5, which the Giants won 6-4 en route to their second World Championship in three years. The next season's Wild Card Game appearance, in which Johnny Cueto lasted just 3.1 innings in a loss to division rival Pittsburgh, is the only playoff game they have played since.

With the absence of a present to sell fans, the Reds are left with two options: the future or the past. The past is rich for Cincinnati, at least. The town is the crucible of professional baseball, as next season marks the 150th anniversary of the Red Stockings. The club owns five World Championships and another four pennants. The Big Red Machine of the 1970s was one of baseball's most legendary dynasties, responsible for four of the 10 National League titles and the 1975 and 1976 World Series victories.

But now, a large portion of Reds fans—and Cincinnati area denizens in general—are too young to remember the Big Red Machine as anything but legend, and a substantial amount are too young to even remember the 1990 World Champions, the last great Reds team. A 35-year-old Reds fan experienced that one great Reds squad was when he was all of seven years old. Their kids? Forget it. Flags may technically fly forever, but history becomes a hard sell to those whose lived experiences tell them the Reds are an also-ran. The empty seats at GABP these days—sometimes half or more of the total capacity—represent a lost generation of Reds fans.

Cincinnati Reds 2019

So the answer, really, is that they aren't selling much of anything at Great American Ball Park these days, unless you're a huge fan of Skyline Chili and $8 beers. Since 2005, when the ownership group led by Robert Castellini purchased the team from Carl Lindner for $270 million, the Reds have been the perfect example of how you don't actually need to sell baseball to make money off a baseball team. Only in 2013 and 2014, as the Reds tried desperately to hold the core of their early-decade success together, did the Reds get into the top half of MLB payrolls. Since then, the club's motto has been sell-sell-sell, as 2016 and 2017 marked their lowest payrolls of the decade (both under $100 million) and their lowest ranks in year-end payroll (28th and 25th, respectively) as far back as Cot's Contracts has tracked such data.

Lindner is a good example himself. He bought the Cincinnati Reds from Marge Schott in 1999 for $67 million. As owner, Lindner presided over six seasons, in which the Reds started as 96-win team and plummeted to losing at least 85 games in four straight campaigns. For those services rendered, Lindner walked away with a nearly 400 percent profit. Castellini's reign has been similarly lucrative. Even with attendance plummeting and the franchise stagnating, Forbes still pegs the value of the Reds at just over one billion dollars. Decent gig if you can get it.

A staggering amount of that value is entirely independent of the product the Reds put on the field. The terms of Cincinnati's new deal with Fox Sports Ohio were never disclosed, although we do know the team received an equity stake in the network. There are over 2 million cable households in Ohio, and thanks to bundled cable packages, most are subscribers to FSO. Even though Reds TV ratings were surprisingly high in 2018, they still reached all of 35,000 homes, meaning the rest of those cable TV households—roughly half the state—are footing that bill and contributing to the value of the Reds through that equity stake as well.

Revenue sharing checks also have no correlation with the win column, and league-wide revenue continues to balloon. The league passed the $10 billion mark for the first year in 2018. The MLB Players Association has already started coming after clubs for failing to use their revenue sharing checks for competitive purposes, namely the Rays, Marlins and Pirates. The Reds have only recently seen their payrolls reach similar lows to those culprits, and they don't have the history of cynical behavior the Rays and Marlins in particular have exhibited, but they could be next if the pattern doesn't change.

But the worst grift of all is the stadium. Of the $325 million price tag, $286 million came from a regressive sales tax on Hamilton County residents. The Reds insisted on a new stadium within three decades of the construction of Riverfront Stadium, Cincinnati's home beginning in 1970. Was it even necessary? Riverfront's astroturf was always an eyesore, but the Cincinnati Business Courier reported in 1996 that the stadium's manager estimated it would take just $100 million to take the multi-purpose stadium (once home of both the Reds and the NFL's Cincinnati Bengals) and optimize it for baseball. The Reds declined that option, even though the city would have paid for all of Riverfront's renovations and was asking for a $45 million payment from the Reds for Great American Ball Park.

It makes sense, though, given that the stadium is the crown jewel of the Reds portfolio of assets. According to Forbes, Great American Ball Park accounts for $175 million of that $1.01 billion valuation of the Reds. Given that the Marlins sold for $1.2 billion and certainly offer nothing but their fancy new stadium, that estimate may be low. Between the passive value provided by the stadium, cable TV and revenue sharing, though, it's clear the Reds and other small-market teams around the country don't have to try to make money. When you profit simply by owning a baseball team, where is the incentive to push a rebuild?

I understand the competitive arguments for the protracted rebuilds like the one on which the Reds have embarked. I'm not convinced they will continue to work. The strategy breaks down when the strategy becomes en vogue. The Astros signed four top-five picks between 2012 and 2015, and two of them—Carlos Correa and Alex Bregman—have become franchise cornerstones. The Royals brief burst of success was fueled by four top-five picks between 2005 and 2008. All four—Alex Gordon, Mike Moustakas, Eric Hosmer and Luke Hochevar—were contributors to the 2015 World Champion Royals squad.

The Reds picked second in both 2016 and 2017, but they will pick just seventh in 2019 because nearly a third of the league threw in the towel on day one of the regular season, just as the Reds did. I don't think the Reds can reasonably compete in 2019, and if the goal is a championship, the focus has to be on the future. But waiting to lose and amass the draft picks necessary for the kind of Prospect Wave that is supposed to make those years of losing pay off becomes less and less viable the more teams are gunning—or falling flat on their faces—for those top picks.

Lest we forget, what made Moneyball compelling as a sports narrative isn't that it's possible to build a cheaper, more efficient baseball team. What was compelling was seeing the possibility of winning from an apparent losing position through intelligence and cunning, and through finding what nobody else even thought to look for. These copycat rebuilding efforts will proclaim their intelligent approach and how we must trust their Process, but they aren't doing anything we—or their opponents—haven't seen before.

Branch Rickey wrote in his 1965 autobiography that ownership must eliminate the signing bonus in order to curb competition among teams, competition Rickey thought would destroy the profitability of baseball. Thus, the draft, which more than succeeded in driving down the cost of amateur talent. The real problem Rickey was solving was the problem of competition. In 1964, the bidding on top prospect Rick Reichardt ended with the Angels signing him to a $205,000 bonus. The next year, Rick Monday received $100,000 from the Mets as the #1 draft pick. The effects of competition—or the lack thereof—are apparent.

What we have seen over the last 30 years or so since Bud Selig and his cohort of small-market allies rose to power is the erosion of avenues for teams to compete for talent. Want to sign top or mid-level free agents? Better be prepared to sacrifice draft picks. Want to get creative with leveraging free agent compensation for draft picks like the Rays and Blue Jays did? They'll restructure the compensation system to prevent it. Want to spend more on international free agents, amateur or otherwise? Better be prepared to pay huge taxes. Want to go over slot and add impact talent in the draft? More taxes.

Those strategies gave real hope that the system could be beaten. Naturally, major league owners—including the small market owners these rules restrict the most—have relentlessly struck them down over the last half-decade. Instead, these rules lead to a system where talent is passively distributed, according to slots and budgets and caps, rather than fought for.

It may sound counterintuitive, but this is the ideal setup for baseball owners—especially the small-market cohort. They, after all, are the ones who pushed hardest for these rules. These owners are happy to take their turns at competition whenever the prospect waves arrive as long as they can justify miniscule payrolls in the interim by calling it their Process. Want us to sign a free agent? Make a big splash in the draft or with international amateurs? Well, that wouldn't be prudent. Just don't ask us about how we made it that way.

For what Ohioans are paying—from ticket prices to the stadium cost to their cable bills—they deserve more than austerity-level baseball. Ohio is rich with other sports options for fans who are tired of the same-old same-old Reds, whether it's the other professional teams in Cincinnati or up the road in Cleveland, or the myriad college teams in the state and in nearby northern Kentucky or Indiana. The Reds, after nearly three decades of mediocrity, can't skate by on the clout of Major League Baseball. They have to offer something, or that lost generation of fans will turn into two as others ditch the Reds for the Indians, for hockey, for football, for basketball, or for something else entirely.

I hope, for the sake of Reds fans and for baseball fans in small markets everywhere, who are constantly being left behind by baseball's powers that be, that the system changes eventually, whether in the 2021 CBA or beyond. Cincinnati is a town with a nearly unparalleled baseball history and a thirst for winning. But as it exists right now, there is no incentive for Castellini or whatever hedge fund eventually buys the team from him to change the plan. It is working out quite well for him, and second lost generation of fans or not, the profits will keep flowing his way by design. Welcome to Major League Baseball, a magical world where failure is success and cities like Cincinnati are the losers because of it.

—*Jack Moore is a freelance sports and video game writer in Minneapolis, MN.*

Part 2: Player Analysis

Tucker Barnhart C

Born: 01/07/91   Age: 28   Bats: B   Throws: R
Height: 5'11"   Weight: 192   Origin: Round 10, 2009 Draft (#299 overall)

YEAR	TEAM	LVL	AGE	PA	R	2B	3B	HR	RBI	BB	K	SB	CS	AVG/OBP/SLG
2016	CIN	MLB	25	420	34	23	1	7	51	36	72	1	0	.257/.323/.379
2017	CIN	MLB	26	423	26	24	2	7	44	42	68	4	0	.270/.347/.403
2018	CIN	MLB	27	522	50	21	3	10	46	54	96	0	4	.248/.328/.372
2019	CIN	MLB	28	449	48	22	2	10	50	44	82	2	1	.263/.341/.405

Breakout: 5%   Improve: 49%   Collapse: 6%   Attrition: 21%   MLB: 96%
Comparables: Dioner Navarro, Josh Thole, Clint Courtney

A consistently above-average catcher over the three previous seasons, the Reds finally gave the full weight of catching duties to Barnhart in 2018. And while his offense remained as consistent as ever, the bottom fell out of his defense due to a combination of the third-worst framing in baseball and a precipitous drop from throwing out 44 percent of would-be stealers to a career-low 24 percent. Even a catcher of his 2018 pedigree is still a bargain at the rate at which he was extended, but a second year of depreciating skill behind the plate could turn the tables quickly. After all, Barnhart has never been even an average hitter by DRC+. A solid line-drive rate and improving contact quality means Barnhart has a good chance to mask his depreciation with a batting average bounce back, but he doesn't exactly excel in the sleight of hand.

YEAR	TEAM	P. COUNT	FRM RUNS	BLK RUNS	THRW RUNS	TOT RUNS
2016	CIN	16074	-2.3	2.3	1.7	1.8
2017	CIN	15640	-8.2	2.7	4.9	-0.9
2018	CIN	16826	-11.5	3.6	-0.3	-8.4
2019	CIN	16753	-10.0	2.8	1.4	-5.9

YEAR	TEAM	LVL	AGE	PA	DRC+	VORP	BABIP	BRR	FRAA	WARP
2016	CIN	MLB	25	420	87	14.6	.299	-1.7	C(108): 3.4	1.6
2017	CIN	MLB	26	423	90	20.8	.312	-1.6	C(110): 0.7	1.5
2018	CIN	MLB	27	522	86	12.1	.291	-3.3	C(118): -9.6, 1B(11): -0.7	0.2
2019	CIN	MLB	28	449	96	17.5	.306	-0.8	C -6	1.0

Tucker Barnhart, continued

Batted Ball Distribution

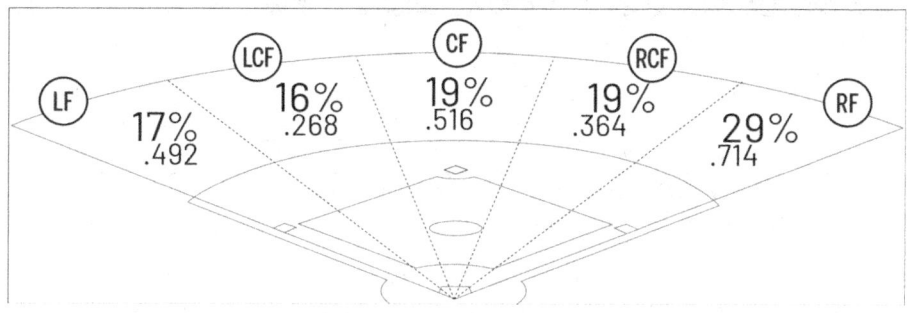

Strike Zone vs LHP

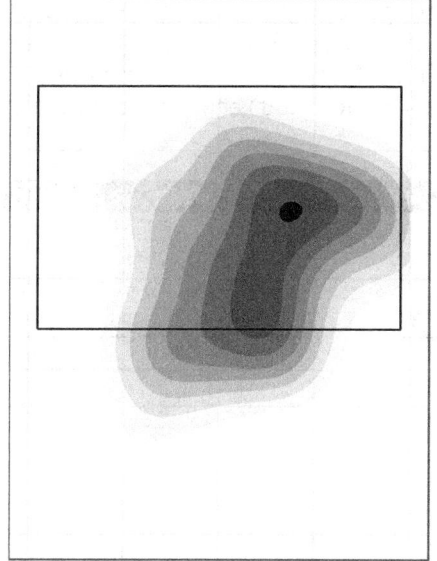

Strike Zone vs RHP

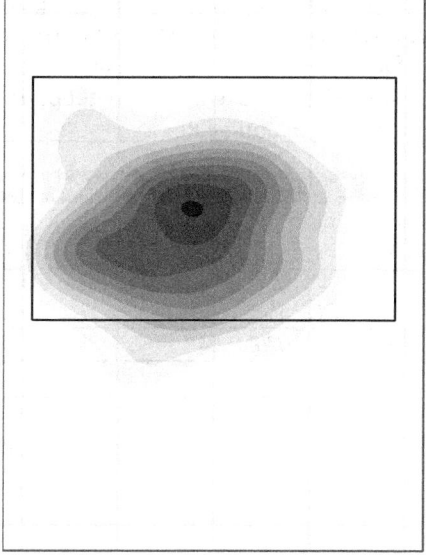

Alex Blandino INF

Born: 11/06/92   Age: 26   Bats: R   Throws: R
Height: 6'0"   Weight: 190   Origin: Round 1, 2014 Draft (#29 overall)

YEAR	TEAM	LVL	AGE	PA	R	2B	3B	HR	RBI	BB	K	SB	CS	AVG/OBP/SLG
2016	PEN	AA	23	465	52	18	0	8	37	55	114	14	5	.232/.333/.337
2017	PEN	AA	24	236	31	22	0	6	31	32	49	3	4	.259/.374/.462
2017	LOU	AAA	24	237	29	14	1	6	20	32	37	1	3	.270/.390/.444
2018	CIN	MLB	25	147	14	4	0	1	8	13	41	0	0	.234/.324/.289
2019	CIN	MLB	26	99	11	5	0	2	10	10	23	1	0	.230/.320/.356

Breakout: 4%   Improve: 24%   Collapse: 5%   Attrition: 23%   MLB: 44%
Comparables: Taylor Green, Rob Refsnyder, Kory Casto

Blandino saw his season end early due to a knee injury, but given how often he takes a walk, he should be able to kick up his rehab by taking a lot of strolls to first base. In his short stint with the Reds, he was perhaps too passive, as he paired an extremely good ability to hold his swing on balls with an extremely bad swing rate on pitches in the zone. He does make a lot of contact when he chooses to engage the ball, but his power doesn't project to get to average and his speed won't be an asset. Defensively, he fits best at second base, but since he faces an uphill battle to stay in one spot, the fact that he can move around the infield will make help him get plate appearances and keep him from putting down roots in Louisville.

YEAR	TEAM	LVL	AGE	PA	DRC+	VORP	BABIP	BRR	FRAA	WARP
2016	PEN	AA	23	465	96	12.2	.302	-2.0	2B(74): -5.1, 3B(30): 1.2	-0.3
2017	PEN	AA	24	236	132	12.9	.315	-1.6	2B(39): 1.8, 3B(18): 2.1	1.3
2017	LOU	AAA	24	237	136	11.9	.305	-2.8	2B(29): -1.8, 3B(26): 0.5	1.1
2018	CIN	MLB	25	147	79	2.7	.337	2.3	2B(21): -1.4, 3B(15): -1.2	0.0
2019	CIN	MLB	26	99	88	2.0	.299	-0.2	2B -1, SS 0	0.1

Alex Blandino, continued

Batted Ball Distribution

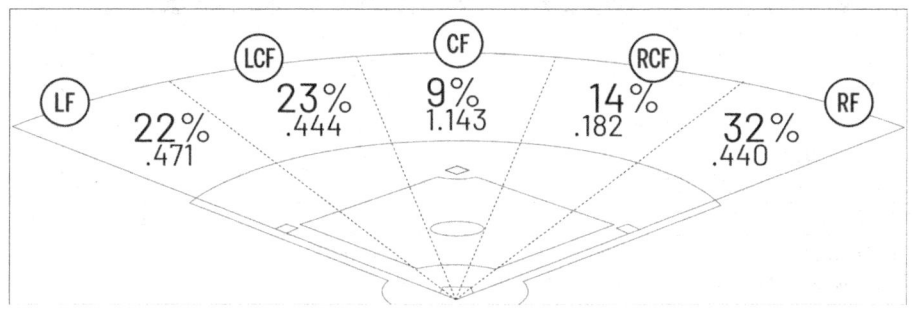

Strike Zone vs LHP

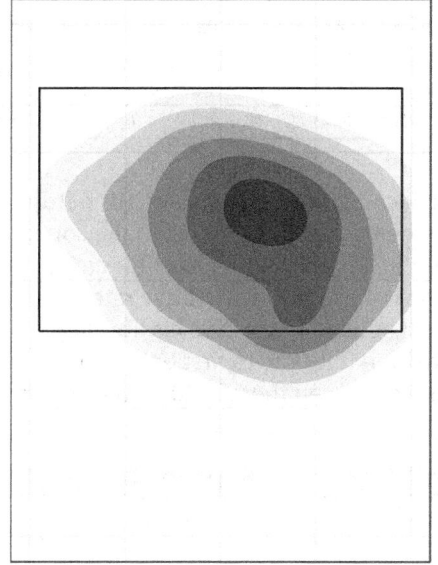

Strike Zone vs RHP

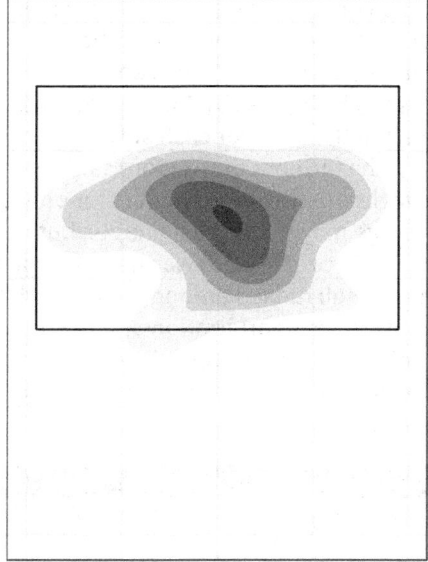

Curtis Casali C

Born: 11/09/88   Age: 30   Bats: R   Throws: R
Height: 6'3"   Weight: 235   Origin: Round 10, 2011 Draft (#317 overall)

YEAR	TEAM	LVL	AGE	PA	R	2B	3B	HR	RBI	BB	K	SB	CS	AVG/OBP/SLG
2016	DUR	AAA	27	81	5	1	0	2	15	15	12	0	0	.254/.407/.365
2016	TBA	MLB	27	256	23	10	0	8	25	25	82	0	0	.186/.273/.336
2017	DUR	AAA	28	343	36	10	0	5	48	37	65	0	0	.263/.351/.347
2017	TBA	MLB	28	13	2	0	0	1	3	3	3	0	0	.333/.462/.667
2018	DUR	AAA	29	104	13	5	0	4	20	7	19	0	0	.274/.327/.453
2018	CIN	MLB	29	156	15	10	0	4	16	12	32	0	2	.293/.355/.450
2019	CIN	MLB	30	146	15	5	0	4	15	13	35	0	0	.231/.303/.362

Breakout: 5%   Improve: 41%   Collapse: 4%   Attrition: 26%   MLB: 60%
Comparables: Chris Gimenez, Dustin Garneau, George Kottaras

After an inauspicious start to the offseason, one final change of scenery certainly looks to have done Casali some good, at least as far as his wallet is concerned. After being caught and released by two AL West teams, stashed in Triple-A by Tampa Bay, and dealt to the Reds for cash at the end of May, the former Commodore saw four straight months in the majors for only the second time in his career. His batting average may not be sustainable, but he made much more contact in the zone; his 86 percent in 2018 was nearly 10 percentage points higher than his career rate. Casali ranked among the top 20 hitters in baseball in line-drive rate. If he wants to get to arbitration and beyond, he'll need to make sure his framing doesn't slip again. Well, either that or transition full-time to first base, a position at which he accumulated a 1.467 OPS while he played there in 2018. Watch out, Joey Votto.

YEAR	TEAM	P. COUNT	FRM RUNS	BLK RUNS	THRW RUNS	TOT RUNS
2016	TBA	9368	6.6	-1.3	0.9	5.5
2017	DUR	7761	2.3	-3.0	-1.0	-1.7
2017	TBA	486	0.6	-0.1	0.0	0.8
2018	CIN	4795	-2.1	-1.3	-0.2	-3.0
2018	DUR	3527	1.8	0.3	-0.3	1.9
2019	CIN	5074	-0.1	-1.0	-0.1	-1.2

YEAR	TEAM	LVL	AGE	PA	DRC+	VORP	BABIP	BRR	FRAA	WARP
2016	DUR	AAA	27	81	130	3.6	.280	-1.1	C(13): 0.2	0.3
2016	TBA	MLB	27	256	73	-0.4	.250	-2.6	C(76): 4.8	0.5
2017	DUR	AAA	28	343	104	9.7	.320	-0.4	C(53): -2.1	0.6
2017	TBA	MLB	28	13	94	3.0	.333	0.3	C(8): 0.6	0.2
2018	DUR	AAA	29	104	111	4.5	.301	-0.1	C(26): 1.0	0.6
2018	CIN	MLB	29	156	101	9.1	.352	0.1	C(38): -4.1, 1B(6): 0.1	0.3
2019	CIN	MLB	30	146	70	1.2	.281	-0.3	C -2	-0.2

Curtis Casali, continued

Batted Ball Distribution

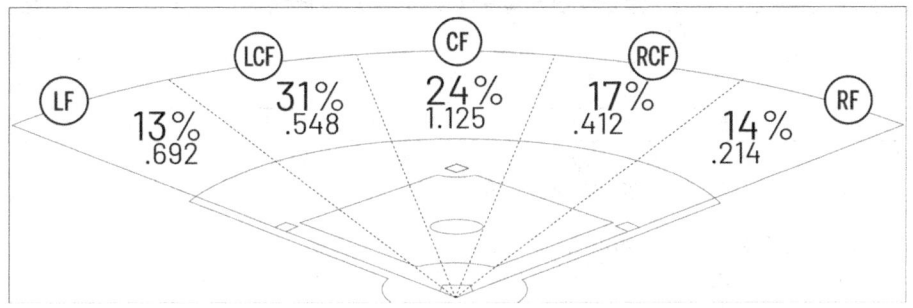

Strike Zone vs LHP

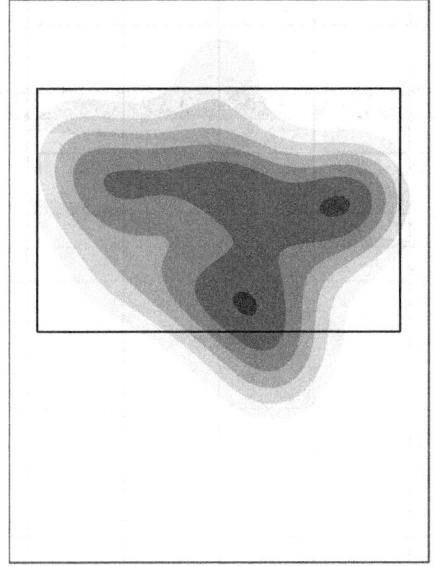

Strike Zone vs RHP

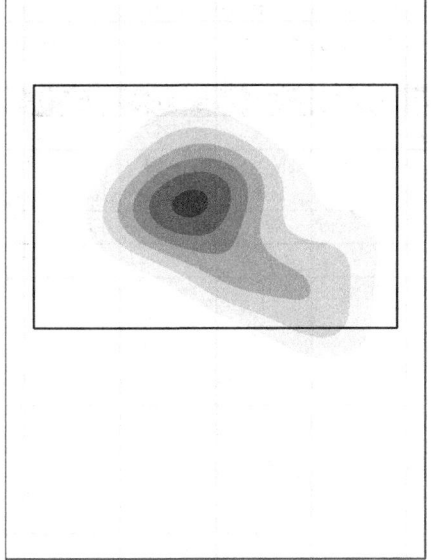

Derek Dietrich LF

Born: 07/18/89   Age: 29   Bats: L   Throws: R
Height: 6'0"   Weight: 205   Origin: Round 2, 2010 Draft (#79 overall)

YEAR	TEAM	LVL	AGE	PA	R	2B	3B	HR	RBI	BB	K	SB	CS	AVG/OBP/SLG
2016	MIA	MLB	26	412	39	20	5	7	42	32	84	1	0	.279/.374/.425
2017	MIA	MLB	27	464	56	22	5	13	53	36	98	0	1	.249/.334/.424
2018	MIA	MLB	28	551	72	26	2	16	45	29	140	2	0	.265/.330/.421
2019	CIN	MLB	29	503	54	24	3	13	58	35	115	1	1	.244/.331/.393

Breakout: 3%   Improve: 37%   Collapse: 9%   Attrition: 6%   MLB: 94%
Comparables: Desmond Jennings, Alex Gordon, Andy Dirks

What made Dietrich valuable in years past — his ability to play all over the infield while being shielded from left-handed pitchers like you shield your children from certain *Game of Thrones* scenes — evaporated. Roster construction and injuries forced Dietrich to play 98 percent of his innings at either first base or in the left field, and he topped 100 plate appearances versus lefties for the first time. Though he turned in an average-at-best season at the plate, he still suffered against lefties and was a legitimate defensive liability at his new positions, leading to a non-tender.

YEAR	TEAM	LVL	AGE	PA	DRC+	VORP	BABIP	BRR	FRAA	WARP
2016	MIA	MLB	26	412	102	29.7	.343	-1.1	2B(75): -0.3, 1B(16): -0.1	1.1
2017	MIA	MLB	27	464	96	22.6	.294	0.5	3B(103): -7.6, 1B(10): -0.3	0.7
2018	MIA	MLB	28	551	100	24.8	.336	1.7	LF(97): -8.4, 1B(33): -1.9	0.4
2019	CIN	MLB	29	503	104	16.2	.310	0.3	LF -4, 1B -1	1.2

Derek Dietrich, continued

Batted Ball Distribution

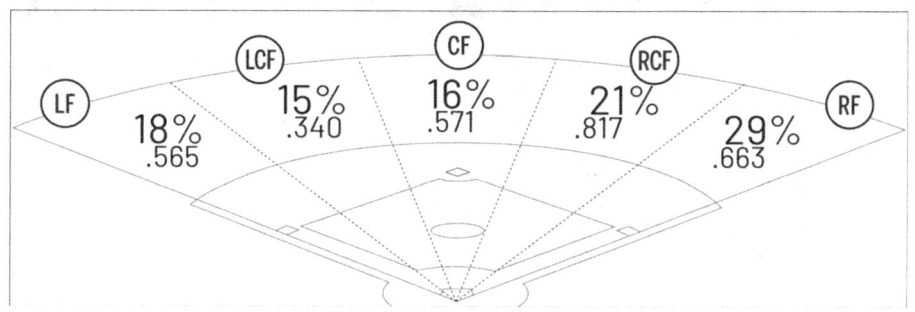

Strike Zone vs LHP

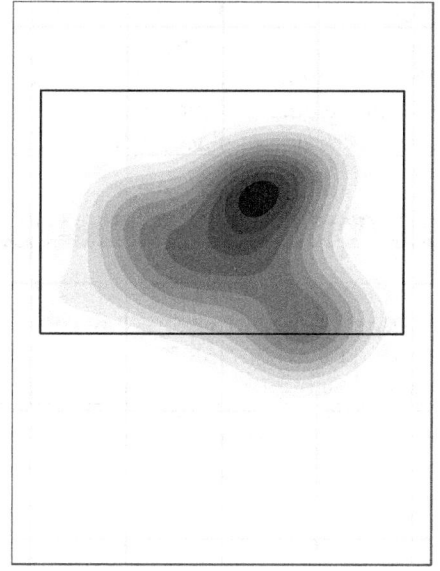

Strike Zone vs RHP

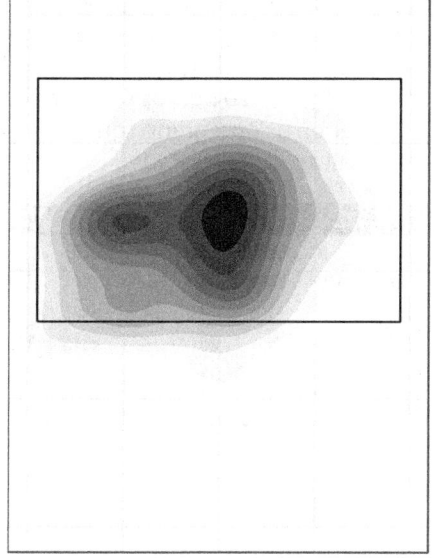

Phil Ervin OF

Born: 07/15/92   Age: 26   Bats: R   Throws: R
Height: 5'10"   Weight: 207   Origin: Round 1, 2013 Draft (#27 overall)

YEAR	TEAM	LVL	AGE	PA	R	2B	3B	HR	RBI	BB	K	SB	CS	AVG/OBP/SLG
2016	PEN	AA	23	505	71	22	3	13	45	65	88	36	10	.239/.362/.399
2017	LOU	AAA	24	408	46	20	2	7	40	37	83	23	6	.256/.328/.380
2017	CIN	MLB	24	64	8	2	0	3	10	4	15	4	1	.259/.317/.448
2018	LOU	AAA	25	202	25	12	4	5	38	20	39	10	7	.289/.373/.491
2018	CIN	MLB	25	247	27	10	1	7	31	20	60	6	1	.252/.324/.404
2019	CIN	MLB	26	154	19	7	1	4	17	13	36	6	2	.239/.312/.391

Breakout: 12%   Improve: 44%   Collapse: 9%   Attrition: 24%   MLB: 71%
Comparables: Max Muncy, Michael Choice, Brandon Jones

The average National League center fielder hit .256/.326/.408 last year, a near-perfect match for Ervin's offensive numbers over half a season in Cincinnati. If he could also flash the defensive chops of an average big-league center fielder the Reds might have the heir to Billy Hamilton on their hands. Unfortunately, Ervin's plus speed has never been able to paper over the bad routes, inaccurate throws, and sketchy instincts that have made him a liability in the great grass sea. At 26 he's not likely to improve. Still, the first-round pick has enough juice in his bat to launch 20 bombs over a full season and would be a nice fourth outfielder on a contending squad, or a perfectly cromulent placeholder for the perpetually rebuilding Reds.

YEAR	TEAM	LVL	AGE	PA	DRC+	VORP	BABIP	BRR	FRAA	WARP
2016	PEN	AA	23	505	129	38.8	.271	1.2	LF(76): 2.5, CF(31): -1.1	2.0
2017	LOU	AAA	24	408	98	7.7	.315	0.6	LF(56): 8.7, CF(40): -3.1	1.0
2017	CIN	MLB	24	64	96	4.6	.300	1.1	CF(9): -0.6, RF(5): -0.4	0.2
2018	LOU	AAA	25	202	131	14.7	.341	-0.8	LF(37): 5.2, CF(8): -0.5	1.3
2018	CIN	MLB	25	247	96	6.2	.310	1.0	LF(39): 0.2, RF(33): -2.7	0.3
2019	CIN	MLB	26	154	89	3.4	.285	0.5	LF 1, CF 0	0.4

Phil Ervin, continued

Batted Ball Distribution

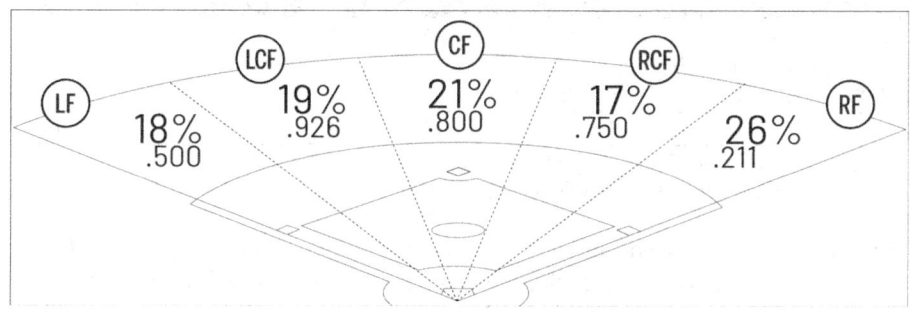

Strike Zone vs LHP

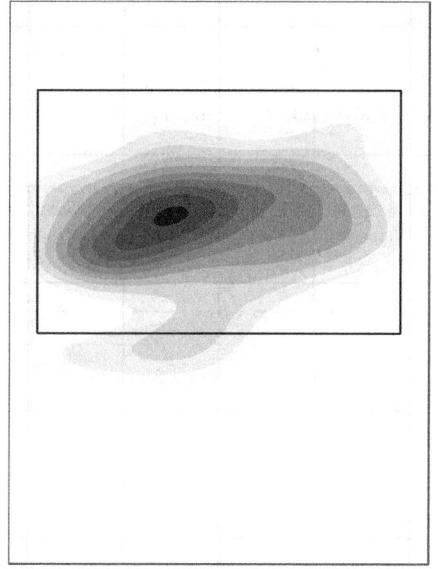

Strike Zone vs RHP

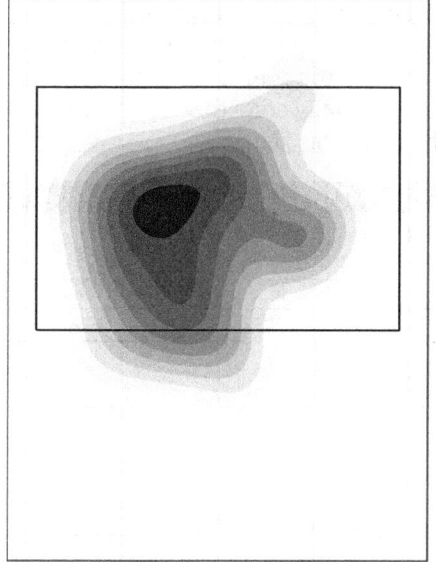

Scooter Gennett 2B

Born: 05/01/90   Age: 29   Bats: L   Throws: R
Height: 5'10"   Weight: 185   Origin: Round 16, 2009 Draft (#496 overall)

YEAR	TEAM	LVL	AGE	PA	R	2B	3B	HR	RBI	BB	K	SB	CS	AVG/OBP/SLG
2016	MIL	MLB	26	542	58	30	1	14	56	38	114	8	1	.263/.317/.412
2017	CIN	MLB	27	497	80	22	3	27	97	30	114	3	2	.295/.342/.531
2018	CIN	MLB	28	638	86	30	3	23	92	42	125	4	2	.310/.357/.490
2019	CIN	MLB	29	571	70	29	3	21	77	41	124	4	2	.286/.342/.474

Breakout: 1%   Improve: 47%   Collapse: 13%   Attrition: 7%   MLB: 100%
Comparables: Howie Kendrick, Aaron Hill, Jimmie Reese

"Gennett is still young enough to develop more power or refine his approach…with good contact skills, a low walk rate and an indifferent glove." That's what we wrote prior to his 2013 rookie season, so color us unsurprised that Scooter's refined approach has led to better pitches to drive, 50 bombs over the last two years, an All-Star berth and a perch among the league's best second sackers. (Okay, so we redacted the part where we compared Gennett to Aaron Miles and his 19 career home runs, so perhaps we're a little surprised.) Last year he stood in well against same-side pitchers and held his own in the field, gains that help to round out his portfolio as he nears free agency. The aging curve can be especially cruel to second basemen, but as long as he can barrel up a fastball he'll earn his keep.

YEAR	TEAM	LVL	AGE	PA	DRC+	VORP	BABIP	BRR	FRAA	WARP
2016	MIL	MLB	26	542	88	14.6	.315	-0.8	2B(127): 4.8	1.2
2017	CIN	MLB	27	497	116	32.8	.339	-1.4	2B(99): -8.9, 3B(10): -0.2	1.4
2018	CIN	MLB	28	638	117	41.8	.358	-0.1	2B(142): -4.5	2.8
2019	CIN	MLB	29	571	108	25.4	.335	-0.6	2B -4	2.1

Scooter Gennett, continued

Batted Ball Distribution

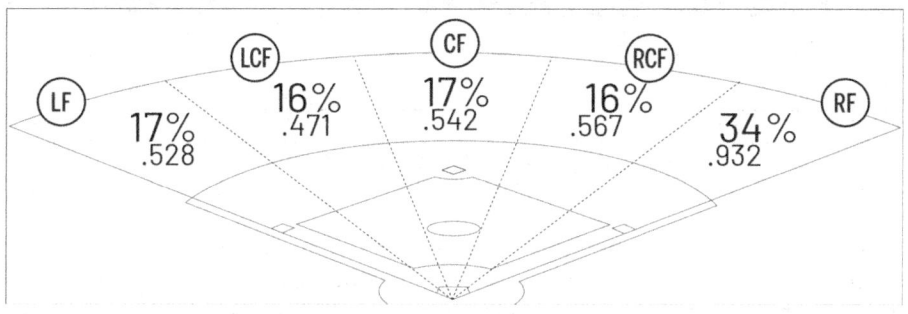

Strike Zone vs LHP

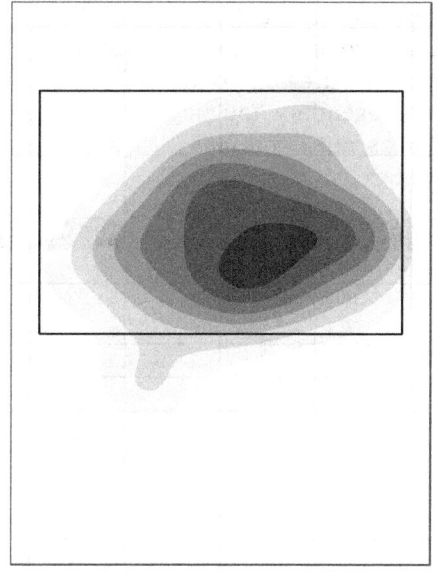

Strike Zone vs RHP

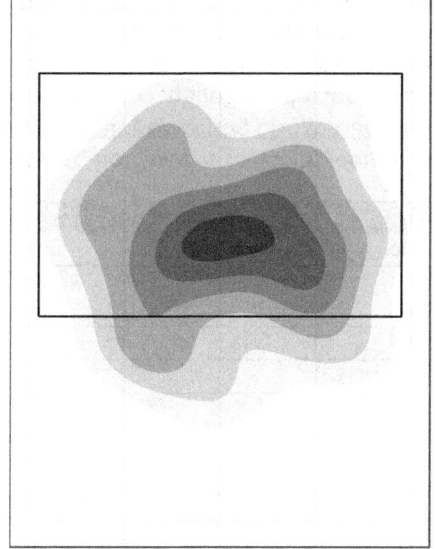

Jose Iglesias SS
Born: 01/05/90 Age: 29 Bats: R Throws: R
Height: 5'11" Weight: 194 Origin: International Free Agent, 2009

YEAR	TEAM	LVL	AGE	PA	R	2B	3B	HR	RBI	BB	K	SB	CS	AVG/OBP/SLG
2016	DET	MLB	26	513	57	26	0	4	32	28	50	7	4	.255/.306/.336
2017	DET	MLB	27	489	56	33	1	6	54	21	65	7	4	.255/.288/.369
2018	DET	MLB	28	464	43	31	3	5	48	19	47	15	6	.269/.310/.389
2019	CIN	MLB	29	444	47	22	2	7	41	29	58	10	5	.251/.308/.368

Breakout: 1% Improve: 49% Collapse: 4% Attrition: 9% MLB: 97%
Comparables: Elvis Andrus, Luis Sojo, Cesar Izturis

On paper, Iglesias is a second-division starter. He avoids strikeouts better than most (fifth-best in the majors last year), though does it without any meaningful line-drive power or a decent walk rate. He grades out fine on defense, although not as well as his reputation would suggest. Beyond the parchment, he's even money to make a breathtaking how-did-he-throw-that play at shortstop. He's right on the cusp of the style outweighing the substance because his level of defense is unteachable and makes the other side work for his outs. He falls somewhere between Rey Ordonez and Omar Vizquel on the one-dimensional shortstop spectrum. Keep in mind, not all players are built to win championships; highlight reels are almost as legendary. You may not remember who every World Series-winning shortstop was, but Tigers fans will sure as rain remember Iglesias throwing off balance to start a double play.

YEAR	TEAM	LVL	AGE	PA	DRC+	VORP	BABIP	BRR	FRAA	WARP
2016	DET	MLB	26	513	79	8.6	.276	1.2	SS(136): 14.2	2.6
2017	DET	MLB	27	489	72	4.4	.285	3.7	SS(130): -4.8	0.4
2018	DET	MLB	28	464	93	18.3	.291	1.6	SS(122): 4.7	2.3
2019	CIN	MLB	29	444	83	9.6	.275	1.4	SS 4	1.4

Jose Iglesias, continued

Batted Ball Distribution

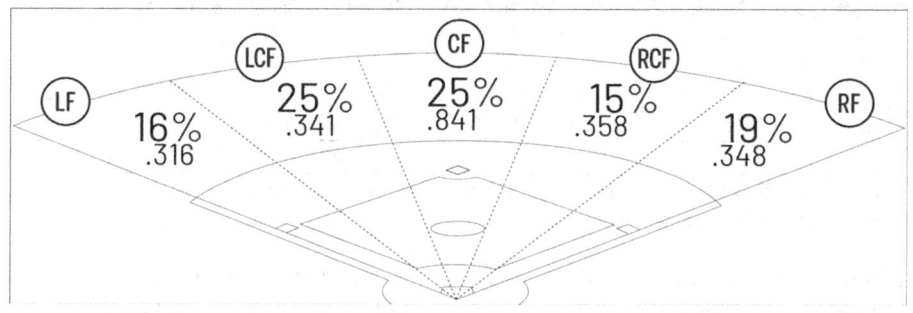

Strike Zone vs LHP **Strike Zone vs RHP**

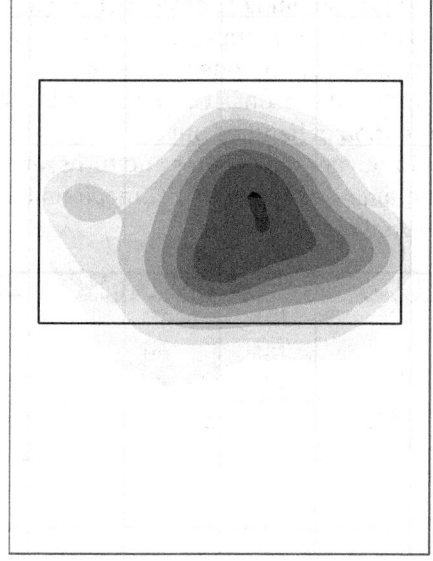

Cincinnati Reds 2019

Matt Kemp RF
Born: 09/23/84   Age: 34   Bats: R   Throws: R
Height: 6'4"   Weight: 210   Origin: Round 6, 2003 Draft (#181 overall)

YEAR	TEAM	LVL	AGE	PA	R	2B	3B	HR	RBI	BB	K	SB	CS	AVG/OBP/SLG
2016	SDN	MLB	31	431	54	24	0	23	69	16	100	0	0	.262/.285/.489
2016	ATL	MLB	31	241	35	15	0	12	39	20	56	1	0	.280/.336/.519
2017	ATL	MLB	32	467	47	23	1	19	64	27	99	0	2	.276/.318/.463
2018	LAN	MLB	33	506	62	25	0	21	85	36	115	0	0	.290/.338/.481
2019	CIN	MLB	34	265	30	14	1	9	34	20	61	1	0	.269/.325/.446

Breakout: 1%   Improve: 15%   Collapse: 23%   Attrition: 25%   MLB: 91%
Comparables: Jim Rice, Garret Anderson, Alfonso Soriano

When the Dodgers acquired Kemp in December 2017, it's unlikely they immediately started cutting a highlight video set to the popular Diddy ditty "Coming Home" to play on Opening Day. In reality, the deal was consummated as a swap of bad contracts with the hopes of lessening the team's luxury-tax burden. Rumors of a Spring Training release swirled, but Kemp responded in the best way, winning a roster spot and hitting .310/.352/.522 in the first half to earn his third All-Star appearance. The second half didn't go as well, but the former franchise cornerstone did manage to stay upright in the field, unlike the last handful of seasons. It's a luxury to be able to trade for a pricey slugger with the intention of handing out an immediate pink slip. It's an even bigger luxury when said slugger rejuvenates and turns into a legit asset, making the $22 million remaining on his 2019 contract infinitely more palatable—and for a middling-payroll squad no less.

YEAR	TEAM	LVL	AGE	PA	DRC+	VORP	BABIP	BRR	FRAA	WARP
2016	SDN	MLB	31	431	107	11.0	.288	-0.4	RF(97): -5.3	0.6
2016	ATL	MLB	31	241	112	18.3	.316	1.5	LF(54): 0.0	1.1
2017	ATL	MLB	32	467	101	7.4	.318	-3.4	LF(103): -14.6	-0.6
2018	LAN	MLB	33	506	116	23.3	.339	-2.1	LF(75): -1.5, RF(51): -2.2	1.6
2019	CIN	MLB	34	265	104	9.4	.318	-0.5	LF -3	0.7

Matt Kemp, continued

Batted Ball Distribution

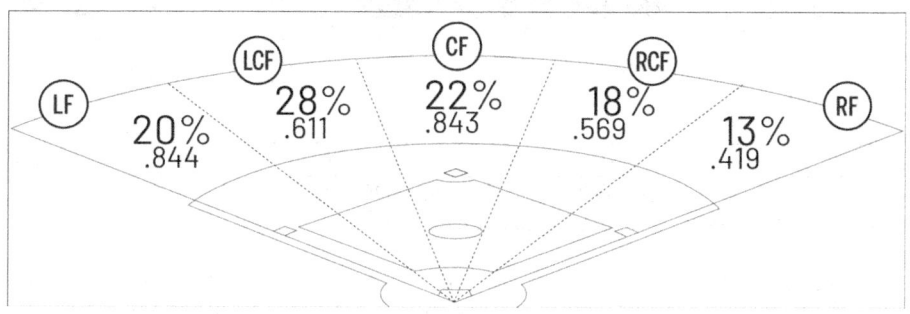

Strike Zone vs LHP

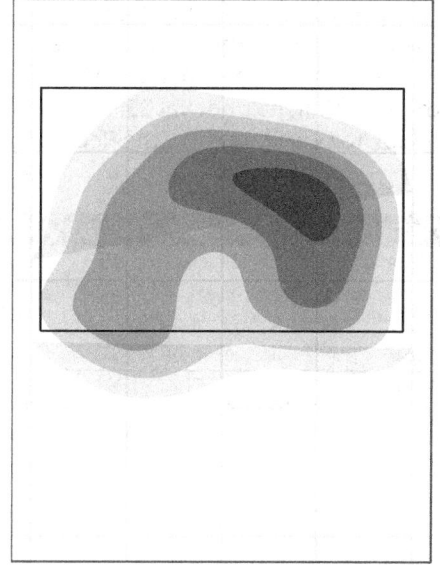

Strike Zone vs RHP

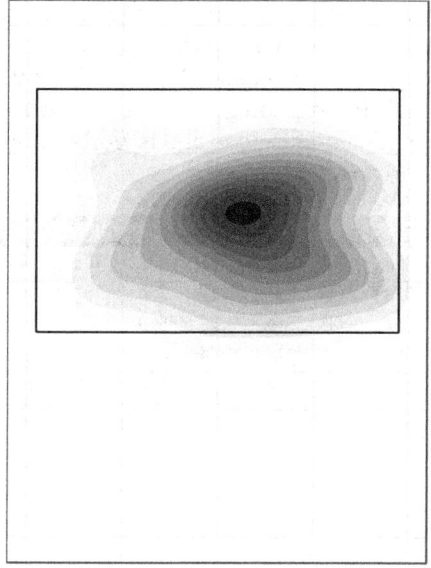

Cincinnati Reds 2019

Jose Peraza SS
Born: 04/30/94   Age: 25   Bats: R   Throws: R
Height: 6'0"   Weight: 196   Origin: International Free Agent, 2010

YEAR	TEAM	LVL	AGE	PA	R	2B	3B	HR	RBI	BB	K	SB	CS	AVG/OBP/SLG
2016	LOU	AAA	22	322	40	15	3	2	21	21	43	10	7	.281/.333/.375
2016	CIN	MLB	22	256	25	8	2	3	25	7	33	21	10	.324/.352/.411
2017	CIN	MLB	23	518	50	9	4	5	37	20	70	23	8	.259/.297/.324
2018	CIN	MLB	24	683	85	31	4	14	58	29	75	23	6	.288/.326/.416
2019	CIN	MLB	25	599	80	25	4	13	55	34	82	25	8	.278/.328/.410

Breakout: 12%   Improve: 80%   Collapse: 5%   Attrition: 14%   MLB: 99%
Comparables: Yuniesky Betancourt, Erick Aybar, Alcides Escobar

Peraza's first season as Cincinnati's full-time shortstop came in like a lamb (.243/.279/.317 through May 25), went out like a lion (.309/.348/.463 the rest of the way), and featured a surprising amount of gopher (14 home runs) in between. Long known as a free-swinging contact hitter with great speed and little thunder, Peraza made a concerted effort to avoid ground balls and raised his power profile from "non-existent" to "occasional." It's fair to question whether he can keep this up, as he continues to rank near the bottom of the league in exit velocity. If some of last year's wall-scrapers start dying at the track, Peraza's offensive value will die with them. Still, he's not yet 25, flashed a fringe-average glove and is worth another look to see if he can be the Reds long-term answer at the six.

YEAR	TEAM	LVL	AGE	PA	DRC+	VORP	BABIP	BRR	FRAA	WARP
2016	LOU	AAA	22	322	105	14.8	.324	1.5	SS(58): -3.6, CF(6): -0.1	0.9
2016	CIN	MLB	22	256	102	10.9	.361	-0.8	SS(31): -1.0, CF(13): -1.3	0.6
2017	CIN	MLB	23	518	76	-0.1	.293	0.6	2B(77): 2.3, SS(55): 0.6	0.7
2018	CIN	MLB	24	683	101	31.2	.307	2.4	SS(156): -3.4, RF(1): 0.0	3.1
2019	CIN	MLB	25	599	92	18.7	.301	2.0	SS -4	1.4

Jose Peraza, continued

Batted Ball Distribution

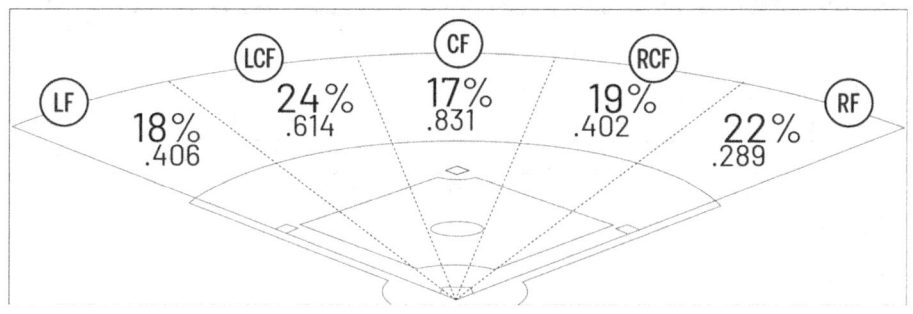

Strike Zone vs LHP   Strike Zone vs RHP

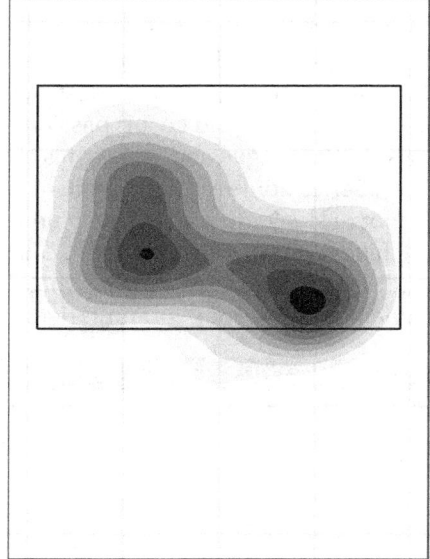

Reds Player Analysis - 39

Yasiel Puig RF

Born: 12/07/90 Age: 28 Bats: R Throws: R
Height: 6'2" Weight: 240 Origin: International Free Agent, 2012

YEAR	TEAM	LVL	AGE	PA	R	2B	3B	HR	RBI	BB	K	SB	CS	AVG/OBP/SLG
2016	OKL	AAA	25	75	12	3	1	4	12	6	8	0	1	.348/.400/.594
2016	LAN	MLB	25	368	45	14	2	11	45	24	74	5	2	.263/.323/.416
2017	LAN	MLB	26	570	72	24	2	28	74	64	100	15	6	.263/.346/.487
2018	LAN	MLB	27	444	60	21	1	23	63	36	87	15	5	.267/.327/.494
2019	CIN	MLB	28	497	70	21	2	21	65	50	95	13	5	.263/.342/.463

Breakout: 1% Improve: 43% Collapse: 9% Attrition: 6% MLB: 97%
Comparables: Andre Ethier, Chet Lemon, Nick Markakis

A Petrarchan sonnet for Yasiel Puig:

    A wild horse gallops across the plains
Power, grace and speed, with limitless joy
In his world, never mistaken for coy
Lacking maturity was a refrain
Once flayed and maligned, now free from those reins
Playing a game made clear he enjoyed
Old unwritten rules, he surely destroyed
Teammates come and go, his passion remains
A wag of the tongue and taste of his bat
World Series home runs and jubilant flips
Try not to love him, you'll have to pretend
Catching runners with what some call a gat
Striding to the plate with a swag that drips
Exuberance is life for #PuigYourFriend

YEAR	TEAM	LVL	AGE	PA	DRC+	VORP	BABIP	BRR	FRAA	WARP
2016	OKL	AAA	25	75	166	5.2	.351	-3.0	RF(17): 0.0	0.2
2016	LAN	MLB	25	368	92	13.7	.306	1.4	RF(90): 5.3, LF(5): 0.0	1.1
2017	LAN	MLB	26	570	119	27.9	.274	-4.3	RF(145): 9.0	3.1
2018	LAN	MLB	27	444	120	23.3	.286	2.4	RF(118): -4.5	1.9
2019	CIN	MLB	28	497	114	23.0	.292	0.3	RF 1	2.4

Yasiel Puig, continued

Batted Ball Distribution

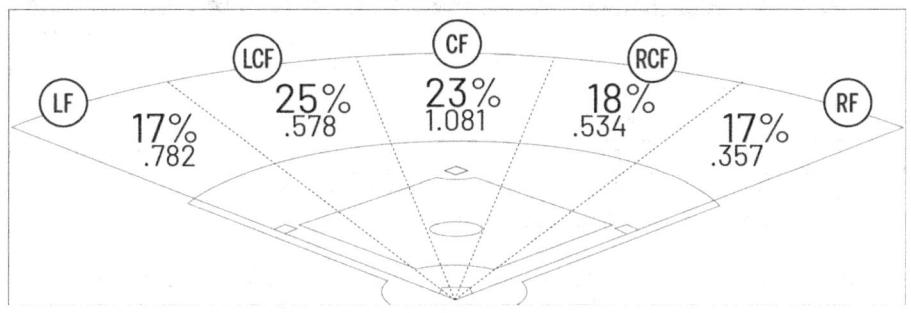

Strike Zone vs LHP

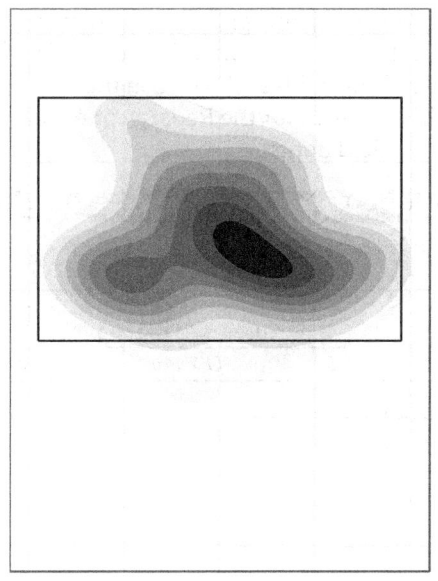

Strike Zone vs RHP

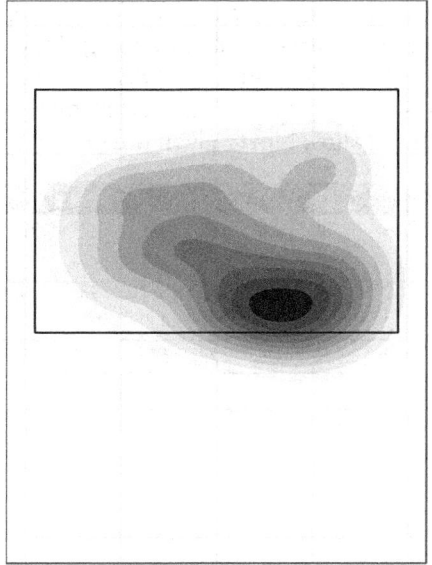

Scott Schebler OF

Born: 10/06/90 Age: 28 Bats: L Throws: R
Height: 6'0" Weight: 228 Origin: Round 26, 2010 Draft (#802 overall)

YEAR	TEAM	LVL	AGE	PA	R	2B	3B	HR	RBI	BB	K	SB	CS	AVG/OBP/SLG
2016	LOU	AAA	25	319	40	18	8	13	43	19	59	2	0	.311/.370/.564
2016	CIN	MLB	25	282	36	12	2	9	40	19	59	2	4	.265/.330/.432
2017	CIN	MLB	26	531	63	25	2	30	67	39	125	5	3	.233/.307/.484
2018	CIN	MLB	27	430	55	19	0	17	49	39	99	4	2	.255/.337/.439
2019	CIN	MLB	28	516	72	23	2	21	63	42	119	5	3	.252/.327/.447

Breakout: 2% Improve: 49% Collapse: 16% Attrition: 22% MLB: 91%
Comparables: Nate Schierholtz, Will Venable, Josh Reddick

On July 13, Schebler was proving those who thought his 2017 season a fluke wrong. He was hitting a cool .278/.351/.470, and while the power was being tampered by a career-low fly-ball rate, his newfound aggressiveness in the zone was helping him squeeze plenty of those extra grounders through the holes. The next day, his aggressiveness in the field would ultimately lead to his undoing. Giving chase to a Yadier Molina fly ball, Schebler ran his right shoulder directly into the outfield wall, sidelining him with a right AC joint sprain for the next six weeks. He limped to the finish line after returning, with a .674 OPS in the season's final month-plus. He'll man left field in 2019 for the Reds, as often as they'll allow him to given their newfound outfield depth.

YEAR	TEAM	LVL	AGE	PA	DRC+	VORP	BABIP	BRR	FRAA	WARP
2016	LOU	AAA	25	319	159	29.9	.352	-1.7	CF(49): 3.1, LF(16): -1.1	2.5
2016	CIN	MLB	25	282	89	10.0	.312	1.7	RF(41): 4.2, CF(18): -2.5	0.6
2017	CIN	MLB	26	531	95	20.6	.248	-0.2	RF(120): -4.8, CF(15): 0.9	0.5
2018	CIN	MLB	27	430	101	14.9	.301	-1.4	RF(86): -2.4, CF(16): 0.5	0.7
2019	CIN	MLB	28	516	100	18.8	.296	-0.5	CF 2, LF 0	2.0

Scott Schebler, continued

Batted Ball Distribution

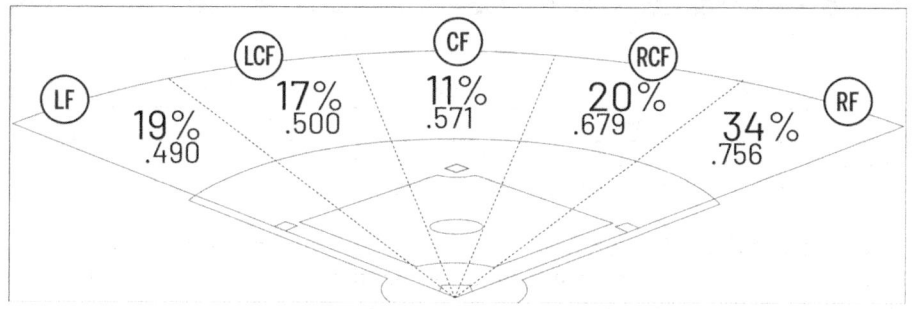

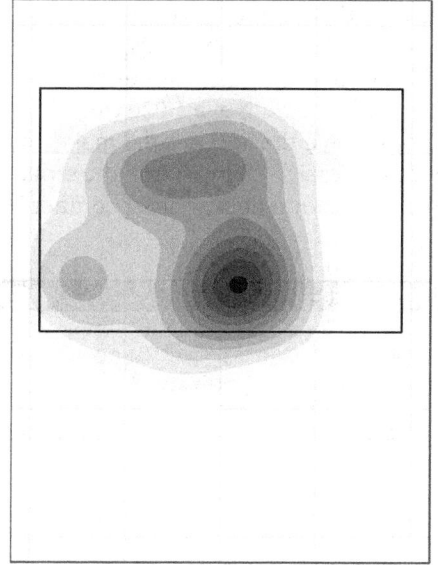

Strike Zone vs LHP

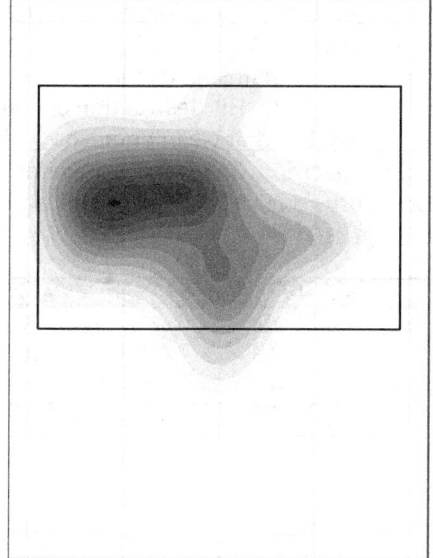

Strike Zone vs RHP

Eugenio Suarez 3B

Born: 07/18/91   Age: 27   Bats: R   Throws: R
Height: 5'11"   Weight: 213   Origin: International Free Agent, 2008

YEAR	TEAM	LVL	AGE	PA	R	2B	3B	HR	RBI	BB	K	SB	CS	AVG/OBP/SLG
2016	CIN	MLB	24	627	78	25	2	21	70	51	155	11	5	.248/.317/.411
2017	CIN	MLB	25	632	87	25	2	26	82	84	147	4	5	.260/.367/.461
2018	CIN	MLB	26	606	79	22	2	34	104	64	142	1	1	.283/.366/.526
2019	CIN	MLB	27	564	74	25	2	23	78	62	131	4	3	.268/.358/.468

Breakout: 8%   Improve: 66%   Collapse: 9%   Attrition: 9%   MLB: 99%
Comparables: Edwin Encarnacion, Kyle Seager, Michael Cuddyer

Pick your metric and Suarez has been improving it for several seasons, at least on offense. He saw gains for the second consecutive year in DRC+, batting average, OPS, line drives and hard-hit rate on fly balls. He's a star, but unfortunately for Suarez, he's about as well-hidden as The Secret Aquarium in Super Mario 64. He finds himself locked in baseball's version of the middle-child syndrome; this is a Reds team that loses too many games to have a second recognizable face, and Joey Votto is locked in at this spot for another half-decade. For the most part, the Venezuela native even went about his improvement in unspectacular fashion. His batted ball profile was nearly identical to 2017. His destruction of southpaws to the tune of a 1.020 OPS continued, but that wasn't not a new phenomenon either. Suarez did make one notable decision, however: he became more aggressive on pitches in the strike zone. Turns out, the trade-off of a handful of walks for reliably harder contact was a good one.

YEAR	TEAM	LVL	AGE	PA	DRC+	VORP	BABIP	BRR	FRAA	WARP
2016	CIN	MLB	24	627	94	19.8	.304	0.7	3B(151): 2.0, SS(2): -0.3	1.9
2017	CIN	MLB	25	632	119	38.8	.309	-4.7	3B(153): -1.9, SS(1): 0.0	3.2
2018	CIN	MLB	26	606	136	45.6	.322	-3.5	3B(143): -7.6, SS(3): 0.0	3.8
2019	CIN	MLB	27	564	119	25.4	.318	-1.1	3B -2	2.3

Eugenio Suarez, continued

Batted Ball Distribution

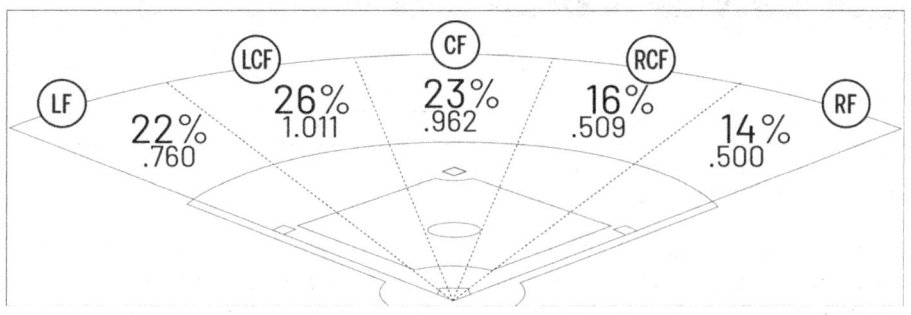

Strike Zone vs LHP

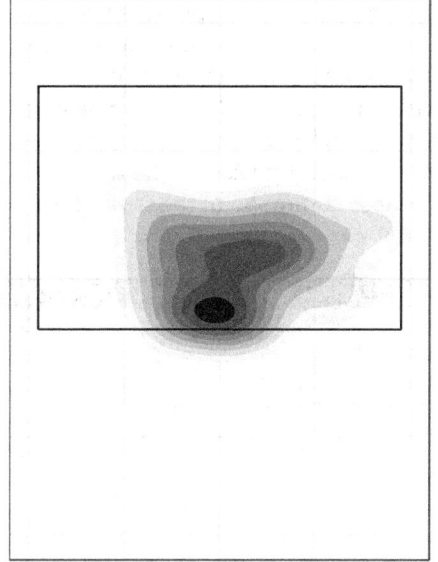

Strike Zone vs RHP

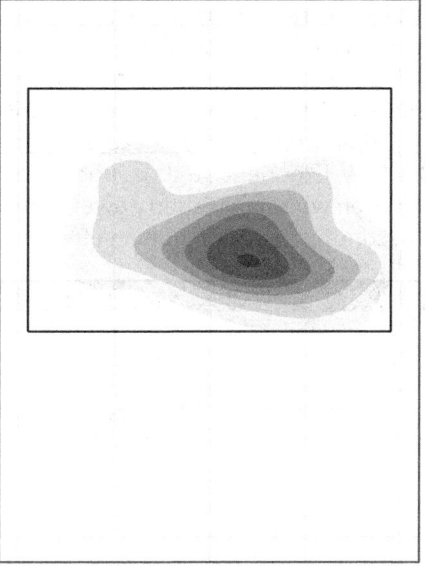

Cincinnati Reds 2019

Joey Votto 1B
Born: 09/10/83   Age: 35   Bats: L   Throws: R
Height: 6'2"   Weight: 220   Origin: Round 2, 2002 Draft (#44 overall)

YEAR	TEAM	LVL	AGE	PA	R	2B	3B	HR	RBI	BB	K	SB	CS	AVG/OBP/SLG
2016	CIN	MLB	32	677	101	34	2	29	97	108	120	8	1	.326/.434/.550
2017	CIN	MLB	33	707	106	34	1	36	100	134	83	5	1	.320/.454/.578
2018	CIN	MLB	34	623	67	28	2	12	67	108	101	2	0	.284/.417/.419
2019	CIN	MLB	35	620	85	33	3	20	83	95	107	4	1	.304/.418/.497

Breakout: 1%   Improve: 28%   Collapse: 18%   Attrition: 6%   MLB: 98%
Comparables: Todd Helton, Edgar Martinez, Albert Pujols

Pitchers beware. Fresh off a disastrous season where Votto plummeted to near the bottom of the top 20 in all of baseball in most measures of offensive performance (including DRC+), the best batsman of his generation has dedicated his offseason to improving what he views as the current weak point in his game: hitting. Although he continued to reach base at a historic clip, last season Votto posted the lowest home run and slugging numbers of his career. His fly-ball rate dropped precipitously from the previous year but was still in line with his career norms, so the lack of thump could be luck, weather, swamp gas reflecting off a weather balloon or the fact Votto has now entered his late thirties. The Master himself blames his conditioning, saying he felt like he was "walking through mud" all season. Pro tip: You feel like that a lot after you turn 35, Joey. Experience tells us not to bet against him hitting 25 dingers this year, but even with diminished power Votto's peerless command of the strike zone will continue to make him an offensive force.

YEAR	TEAM	LVL	AGE	PA	DRC+	VORP	BABIP	BRR	FRAA	WARP
2016	CIN	MLB	32	677	145	58.6	.366	-4.1	1B(154): -1.1	4.1
2017	CIN	MLB	33	707	159	69.9	.321	-6.9	1B(162): 9.5	6.5
2018	CIN	MLB	34	623	124	28.6	.333	-2.6	1B(139): 11.6	3.7
2019	CIN	MLB	35	620	142	40.6	.346	-0.5	1B 6	5.1

Joey Votto, continued

Batted Ball Distribution

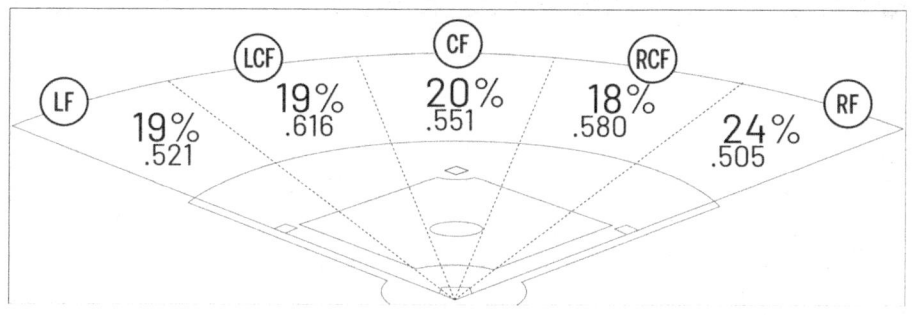

Strike Zone vs LHP   Strike Zone vs RHP

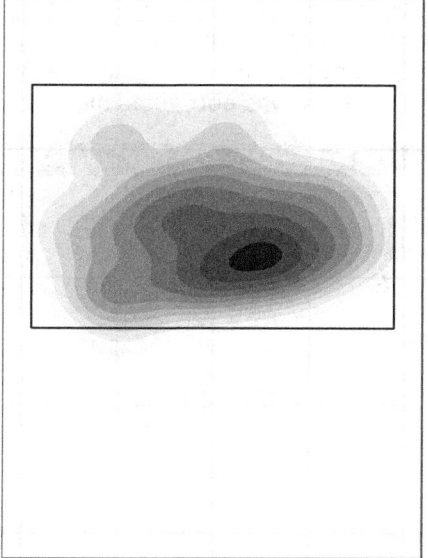

Cincinnati Reds 2019

Mason Williams RF

Born: 08/21/91 Age: 27 Bats: L Throws: R
Height: 6'1" Weight: 195 Origin: Round 4, 2010 Draft (#145 overall)

YEAR	TEAM	LVL	AGE	PA	R	2B	3B	HR	RBI	BB	K	SB	CS	AVG/OBP/SLG
2016	TAM	A+	24	43	2	2	1	0	1	1	4	0	0	.333/.349/.429
2016	SWB	AAA	24	138	19	8	1	0	23	5	21	1	1	.296/.313/.376
2016	NYA	MLB	24	29	4	1	0	0	2	1	12	0	0	.296/.321/.333
2017	NYA	MLB	25	17	3	0	0	0	1	1	2	2	0	.250/.294/.250
2017	SWB	AAA	25	437	44	10	3	2	30	28	66	19	5	.263/.309/.318
2018	LOU	AAA	26	356	52	18	4	6	30	29	57	5	8	.280/.341/.418
2018	CIN	MLB	26	132	10	5	1	2	6	7	29	1	2	.293/.331/.398
2019	CIN	MLB	27	251	28	8	1	5	21	13	52	5	3	.235/.279/.342

Breakout: 5%   Improve: 22%   Collapse: 6%   Attrition: 17%   MLB: 42%
Comparables: Rafael Ortega, Reymond Fuentes, L.J. Hoes

Williams continues to cling to a small chance of being the fifth outfielder on a roster. Don't be deceived by a high batting average in 2018, propped up by a lucky BABIP, because there's almost none of his prospect sheen remaining. The most he offers a major-league roster at this point is the ability to stand in center field without embarrassing himself. Apparently that wasn't quite good enough for the Reds, who outrighted him off the 40-man roster in November.

YEAR	TEAM	LVL	AGE	PA	DRC+	VORP	BABIP	BRR	FRAA	WARP
2016	TAM	A+	24	43	121	0.6	.368	-1.1	CF(4): 0.3	0.0
2016	SWB	AAA	24	138	88	4.1	.343	0.8	CF(18): -1.5, RF(3): -0.2	-0.1
2016	NYA	MLB	24	29	62	0.1	.533	0.3	RF(7): -0.3, CF(2): -0.1	0.0
2017	NYA	MLB	25	17	94	0.0	.286	0.5	CF(5): -0.4, RF(1): -0.1	0.0
2017	SWB	AAA	25	437	71	-4.7	.306	3.3	CF(64): 3.7, LF(19): 0.8	0.0
2018	LOU	AAA	26	356	112	16.5	.324	-1.4	CF(85): -1.9	0.8
2018	CIN	MLB	26	132	84	1.0	.370	0.4	RF(27): -1.7, CF(10): -0.1	-0.1
2019	CIN	MLB	27	251	66	-1.2	.275	-0.2	CF 0, RF 0	-0.1

Mason Williams, continued

Batted Ball Distribution

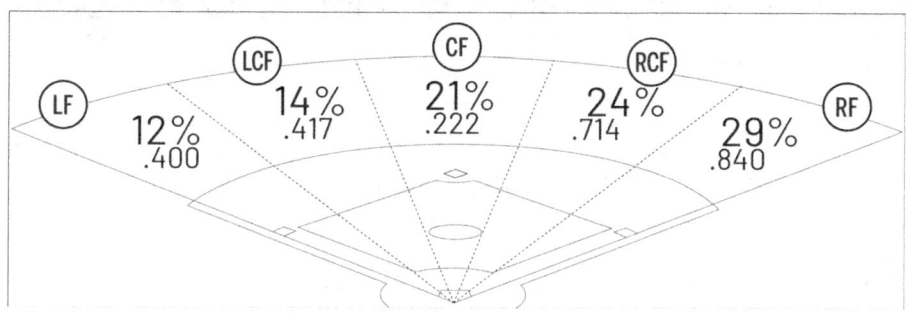

Strike Zone vs LHP

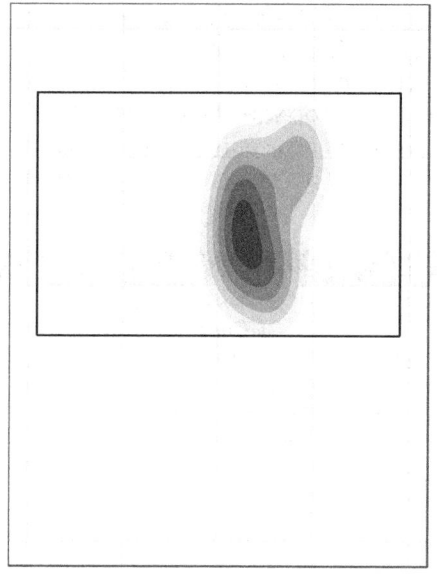

Strike Zone vs RHP

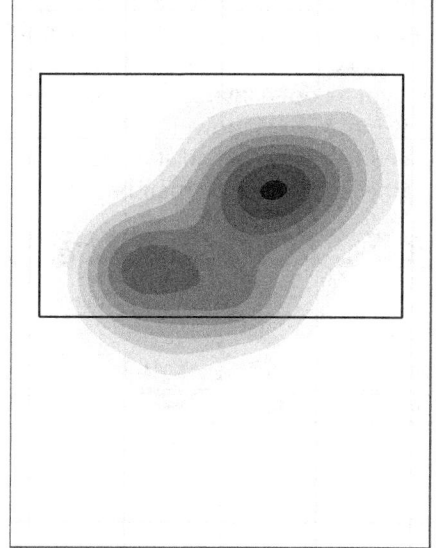

Cincinnati Reds 2019

Jesse Winker RF
Born: 08/17/93   Age: 25   Bats: L   Throws: L
Height: 6'3"   Weight: 215   Origin: Round 1, 2012 Draft (#49 overall)

YEAR	TEAM	LVL	AGE	PA	R	2B	3B	HR	RBI	BB	K	SB	CS	AVG/OBP/SLG
2016	LOU	AAA	22	448	39	22	0	3	45	59	59	0	0	.303/.397/.384
2017	LOU	AAA	23	347	33	22	0	2	41	38	46	2	4	.314/.395/.408
2017	CIN	MLB	23	137	21	7	0	7	15	15	24	1	1	.298/.375/.529
2018	CIN	MLB	24	334	38	16	0	7	43	49	46	0	0	.299/.405/.431
2019	CIN	MLB	25	458	53	22	2	12	54	52	79	1	1	.281/.369/.437

Breakout: 17%   Improve: 49%   Collapse: 4%   Attrition: 14%   MLB: 88%
Comparables: Carlos Quentin, Ramon Flores, Chris Coghlan

Winker's rookie season was a resounding success cut short by surgery to correct a chronic shoulder problem. The former first-round pick proved that he can control the strike zone against major-league pitching by walking more than he whiffed and making consistent hard contact with his smooth lefty stroke. Winker's postage-stamp range confines him to an outfield corner and he rarely packs the wallop associated with success there. Yet there's plenty of reason to think more power will come: his shoulder and wrist may finally be healthy, he's about to enter his prime, launch-angle savants will be whispering in his ear, and he's got an open invitation to spit seeds and talk shop with Joey Votto, who grew into his own power at the same age. If Winker can continue to get on base at a 40-percent clip and starts launching 25 bombs per year, the Reds will have another top-20 bat on their hands.

YEAR	TEAM	LVL	AGE	PA	DRC+	VORP	BABIP	BRR	FRAA	WARP
2016	LOU	AAA	22	448	145	20.4	.347	-1.0	RF(52): 1.0, LF(46): -2.3	2.3
2017	LOU	AAA	23	347	130	14.7	.359	-3.2	RF(70): 2.7, LF(3): 0.4	1.3
2017	CIN	MLB	23	137	112	9.7	.322	-0.6	RF(25): -1.4, LF(2): -0.3	0.3
2018	CIN	MLB	24	334	118	17.2	.336	-2.6	RF(47): -1.0, LF(34): -3.5	0.8
2019	CIN	MLB	25	458	109	17.3	.321	-0.9	LF -2, RF -1	1.4

Jesse Winker, continued

Batted Ball Distribution

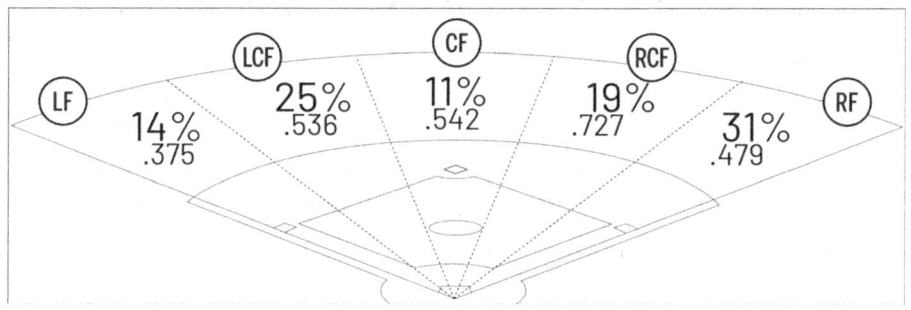

Strike Zone vs LHP

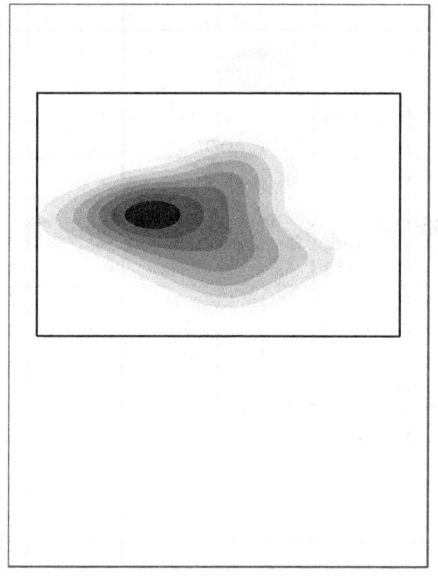

Strike Zone vs RHP

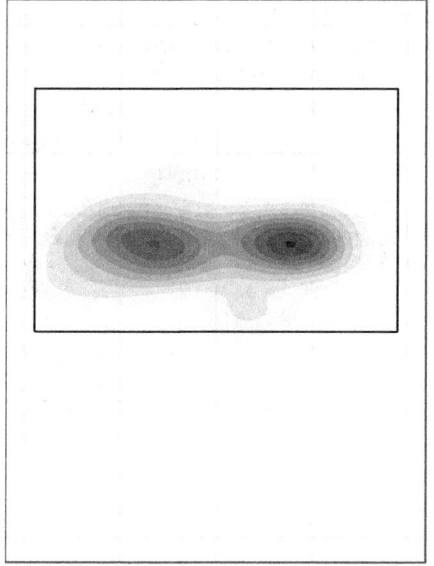

Luis Castillo   RHP

Born: 12/12/92   Age: 26   Bats: R   Throws: R
Height: 6'2"   Weight: 190   Origin: International Free Agent, 2012

YEAR	TEAM	LVL	AGE	W	L	SV	G	GS	IP	H	HR	BB/9	K/9	K	GB%	BABIP
2016	JUP	A+	23	8	4	0	23	21	117^2	95	2	1.4	7.0	91	50%	.271
2016	JAX	AA	23	0	2	0	3	3	14	12	1	4.5	7.7	12	42%	.262
2017	PEN	AA	24	4	4	0	14	14	80^1	68	5	1.5	9.1	81	42%	.293
2017	CIN	MLB	24	3	7	0	15	15	89^1	64	11	3.2	9.9	98	60%	.247
2018	CIN	MLB	25	10	12	0	31	31	169^2	158	28	2.6	8.8	165	48%	.282
2019	*CIN*	*MLB*	*26*	*10*	*9*	*0*	*28*	*28*	*159*	*145*	*20*	*2.7*	*9.2*	*163*	*46%*	*.292*

Breakout: 34%   Improve: 57%   Collapse: 17%   Attrition: 12%   MLB: 90%
Comparables: Taylor Buchholz, Scott Baker, Kris Medlen

While he didn't blossom into an ace last summer, there were plenty of promising signs during Castillo's first full season in the Cincinnati rotation. Armed with a fastball that reaches into the high 90s and a filthy changeup, Castillo shrugged off a rocky April to post a 3.57 ERA thereafter. He held batters to a .232/.286/.408 line the rest of the way while lowering his walk rate and punching out a batter per inning. On the downside, his fly-ball and home run rates soared and lefties that were able to lay off the change tattooed him, slugging .671 against his fastball and sinker. If Castillo can find a way to stop handing out bleacher souvenirs and tame his opposite-handed foes, he has the goods to front the Reds rotation for a long time.

YEAR	TEAM	LVL	AGE	WHIP	ERA	DRA	WARP	MPH	FB%	WHF	CSP
2016	JUP	A+	23	0.96	2.07	2.76	3.6				
2016	JAX	AA	23	1.36	3.86	3.91	0.2				
2017	PEN	AA	24	1.01	2.58	2.81	2.3				
2017	CIN	MLB	24	1.07	3.12	3.41	2.2	98.7	62.1	13.5	47.9
2018	CIN	MLB	25	1.22	4.30	4.76	1.1	97.8	57.2	14.2	48.9
2019	*CIN*	*MLB*	*26*	*1.20*	*3.86*	*3.90*	*2.2*	*97.7*	*59.7*	*14.3*	*49.3*

Luis Castillo, continued

Pitch Shape vs LHH

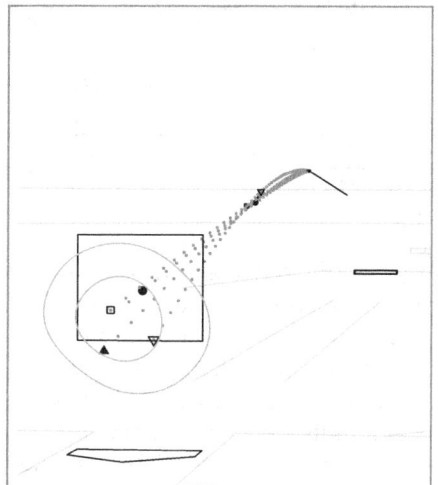

Pitch Shape vs RHH

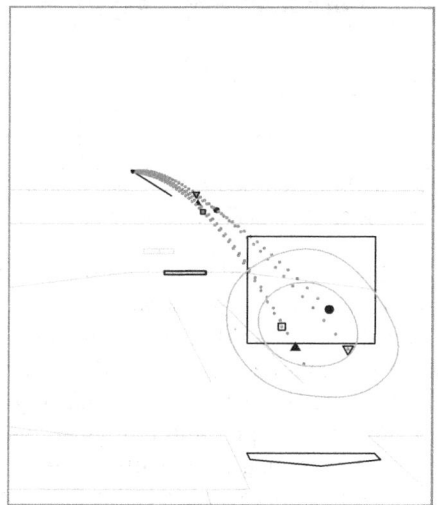

Type	Frequency	Velocity	H Movement	V Movement
● Fastball	35.5%	96.4 [112]	-11 [80]	-14.9 [103]
□ Sinker	21.6%	96.1 [118]	-15.1 [79]	-20.3 [100]
+ Cutter				
▲ Changeup	26.4%	86.8 [106]	-13.8 [86]	-29.9 [93]
× Splitter				
▽ Slider	16.5%	84 [98]	0.9 [83]	-34.5 [96]
◇ Curveball				
⊕ Slow Curveball				
✳ Knuckleball				
▼ Screwball				

Anthony DeSclafani RHP
Born: 04/18/90 Age: 29 Bats: R Throws: R
Height: 6'1" Weight: 195 Origin: Round 6, 2011 Draft (#199 overall)

YEAR	TEAM	LVL	AGE	W	L	SV	G	GS	IP	H	HR	BB/9	K/9	K	GB%	BABIP
2016	LOU	AAA	26	0	1	0	3	3	13	12	4	0.0	7.6	11	46%	.229
2016	CIN	MLB	26	9	5	0	20	20	123^1	120	16	2.2	7.7	105	44%	.295
2018	LOU	AAA	28	0	2	0	2	2	11^1	15	5	1.6	7.9	10	43%	.312
2018	CIN	MLB	28	7	8	0	21	21	115	118	24	2.3	8.5	108	43%	.294
2019	CIN	MLB	29	8	9	0	24	24	144	146	28	3.0	8.8	141	43%	.297

Breakout: 30% Improve: 42% Collapse: 30% Attrition: 13% MLB: 93%
Comparables: Tommy Milone, Jason Vargas, Vance Worley

DeSclafani returned from Tommy John surgery and pitched exactly like the mid-rotation starter he had been in 2016 except for, you know, all those extra runs. The culprit was a ridiculously high rate of home runs per fly ball, a notoriously fickle contagion that afflicted the entire Cincinnati rotation last summer. All of DeSclafani's other peripherals—swinging strike and contact rates; walk, whiff and ground-ball percentages; gum chews per minute—were uncannily similar to his 2016 season, a strange outcome as his pitch mix was notably different. The New Jersey native scrapped his cutter entirely and increased his slider usage by over 700 percent (no, that's not a typo, it jumped from under five percent to nearly 35 percent). Unfortunately, his slider and four-seamer didn't mesh well and hitters didn't let his speedball by them, smacking it around to the tune of a .698 slugging percentage. Like as not, DeSclafani will keep more balls in the park this year, as simply better luck will help return him to his glory days as a no. 4 starter, but a remix of his repertoire will be required to achieve anything more.

YEAR	TEAM	LVL	AGE	WHIP	ERA	DRA	WARP	MPH	FB%	WHF	CSP
2016	LOU	AAA	26	0.92	5.54	3.20	0.3				
2016	CIN	MLB	26	1.22	3.28	4.32	1.5	95.1	55.9	10	47.2
2018	LOU	AAA	28	1.50	6.35	4.55	0.1				
2018	CIN	MLB	28	1.29	4.93	5.16	0.2	95.4	57.9	10.7	49.8
2019	CIN	MLB	29	1.36	4.90	5.01	0.1	94.6	57.1	10.4	48.8

Anthony DeSclafani, continued

Pitch Shape vs LHH

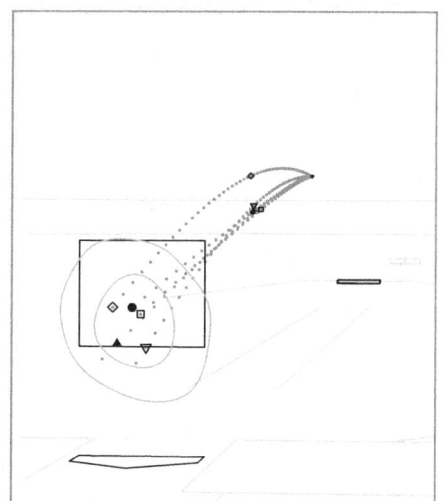

Pitch Shape vs RHH

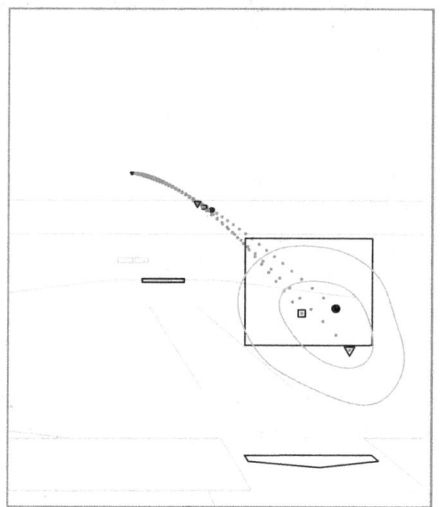

Type	Frequency	Velocity	H Movement	V Movement
● Fastball	31.8%	94.1 [105]	-6.9 [99]	-13.4 [108]
☐ Sinker	26.1%	94.2 [109]	-12.3 [103]	-18.1 [107]
+ Cutter				
▲ Changeup	3.5%	88.9 [114]	-11.8 [97]	-25.2 [106]
✕ Splitter				
▽ Slider	34.8%	87.4 [113]	4.5 [98]	-29.4 [111]
◇ Curveball	3.7%	81.1 [110]	5.8 [92]	-42 [114]
⊕ Slow Curveball				
✻ Knuckleball				
▼ Screwball				

Odrisamer Despaigne   RHP
Born: 04/04/87   Age: 32   Bats: R   Throws: R
Height: 6'0"   Weight: 200   Origin: International Free Agent, 2014

YEAR	TEAM	LVL	AGE	W	L	SV	G	GS	IP	H	HR	BB/9	K/9	K	GB%	BABIP
2016	BAL	MLB	29	0	2	0	16	0	27^1	32	3	4.9	5.6	17	38%	.337
2016	NOR	AAA	29	1	9	0	18	17	88^1	91	5	2.8	7.1	70	53%	.319
2016	MIA	MLB	29	0	0	0	3	0	3	4	0	3.0	0.0	0	50%	.333
2017	NWO	AAA	30	2	4	2	20	10	70	62	6	3.1	6.3	49	52%	.271
2017	MIA	MLB	30	2	3	1	18	8	58^1	57	3	3.7	4.8	31	38%	.280
2018	MIA	MLB	31	2	0	0	11	1	20^1	22	1	3.5	8.0	18	41%	.333
2018	NWO	AAA	31	2	3	2	13	4	43^1	52	0	2.5	8.3	40	44%	.380
2018	ANA	MLB	31	0	3	0	8	4	18^2	30	3	5.3	8.2	17	44%	.415
2019	*CIN*	*MLB*	*32*	*4*	*4*	*1*	*34*	*11*	*80^1*	*83*	*12*	*3.6*	*8.0*	*71*	*44%*	*.316*

Breakout: 15%   Improve: 30%   Collapse: 17%   Attrition: 12%   MLB: 59%
Comparables: Ryan Drese, John Maine, D.J. Carrasco

Despaigne holds the all-time best anagram in baseball: his first and last name transform to "San Diego Padres." He can also rearrange his six different pitches in various sequences, though lately he hasn't quite managed to find a consistent formula to retire batters. His cutter posed the biggest issue among several last year, as his third pitch yielded an unspeakable .483 ISO. Stuck between the rotation, the bullpen and the wrong side of the aging curve, Despaigne will continue to get a handful of innings with his myriad pitches while donning an arrangement of baseball jerseys known only to Calvinists.

YEAR	TEAM	LVL	AGE	WHIP	ERA	DRA	WARP	MPH	FB%	WHF	CSP
2016	BAL	MLB	29	1.72	5.60	7.83	-0.9	95.2	72.9	9.3	45.5
2016	NOR	AAA	29	1.34	3.87	5.51	-0.2				
2016	MIA	MLB	29	1.67	9.00	8.00	-0.1	94.3	72.9	4.2	41.6
2017	NWO	AAA	30	1.23	3.09	3.83	1.3				
2017	MIA	MLB	30	1.39	4.01	5.17	0.2	94.2	84.3	8	47.5
2018	MIA	MLB	31	1.48	5.31	4.61	0.1	94.1	67.4	14.6	43.2
2018	NWO	AAA	31	1.48	4.36	3.90	0.7				
2018	ANA	MLB	31	2.20	8.20	6.74	-0.4	94.9	67.4	9.7	48.9
2019	*CIN*	*MLB*	*32*	*1.43*	*4.74*	*5.13*	*0.0*	*93.5*	*74.7*	*9.7*	*46*

Odrisamer Despaigne, continued

Pitch Shape vs LHH

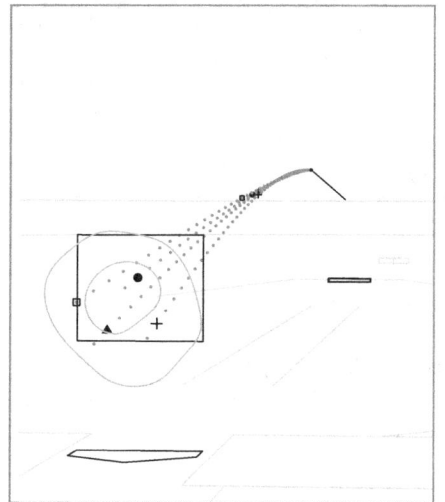

Pitch Shape vs RHH

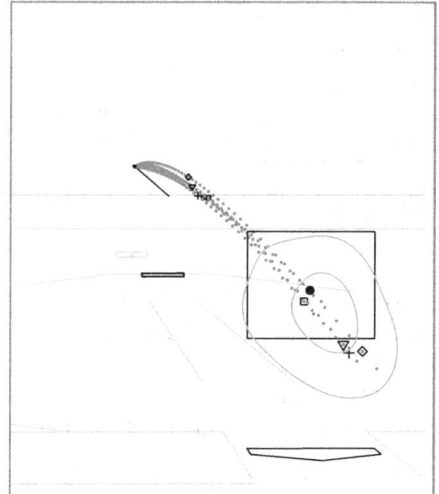

Type	Frequency	Velocity	H Movement	V Movement
● Fastball	23.5%	93.2 [102]	-5.5 [105]	-16.3 [98]
□ Sinker	28.0%	93 [103]	-13.1 [96]	-19.9 [101]
+ Cutter	18.3%	86.3 [85]	3.3 [108]	-30.2 [74]
▲ Changeup	11.2%	80.1 [79]	-6.6 [125]	-28.1 [98]
✕ Splitter				
▽ Slider	10.2%	83.1 [94]	6.6 [108]	-39.2 [82]
◇ Curveball	8.1%	77.3 [96]	10 [109]	-51.6 [92]
✦ Slow Curveball	0.7%	71.6 [107]	8.6 [95]	-66 [101]
✳ Knuckleball				
▼ Screwball				

Reds Player Analysis - 57

Zach Duke LHP

Born: 04/19/83   Age: 36   Bats: L   Throws: L
Height: 6'2"   Weight: 210   Origin: Round 20, 2001 Draft (#594 overall)

YEAR	TEAM	LVL	AGE	W	L	SV	G	GS	IP	H	HR	BB/9	K/9	K	GB%	BABIP
2016	CHA	MLB	33	2	0	1	53	0	37^2	31	2	3.8	10.0	42	65%	.299
2016	SLN	MLB	33	0	1	1	28	0	23^1	17	0	5.0	10.0	26	60%	.293
2017	SLN	MLB	34	1	1	0	27	0	18^1	13	3	2.9	5.9	12	52%	.196
2018	MIN	MLB	35	3	4	0	45	0	37^1	44	0	3.6	9.4	39	60%	.370
2018	SEA	MLB	35	2	1	0	27	0	14^2	13	1	3.7	7.4	12	60%	.286
2019	CIN	MLB	36	2	2	0	36	0	37	37	5	4.5	8.7	36	55%	.300

Breakout: 24%   Improve: 44%   Collapse: 25%   Attrition: 5%   MLB: 77%
Comparables: Fernando Rodney, Scott Eyre, Francisco Cordero

Informed baseball fans are familiar with the process/results matrix: "Good process/good result", "Bad process/Good result", etc. Fans of specific baseball teams root for "good/good" at all times, but for fans of sport and chaos, "bad process/good result", and "good process/bad result" are the very lifeblood the courses through the heart of sports itself.

When healthy, Duke—LOOGY Edition—has spent years performing with minimal variance. The Mariners acquired what appeared to be a very standard, perhaps even above-average Zach Duke at the trade deadline for two non-prospects. It was a fine trade, and naturally what the Mariners received was the worst of all possible Zach Dukes, with nearly a quarter of his appearances resulting in meltdowns. It was a tragic, maybe even unfair result for Seattle. But while small sample size is terrible for analysis, its volatility is maybe one of the reasons we come back to sports again and again. As baseball executives go, Jerry Dipoto seems to be a fairly world-conscious guy. Nonetheless, I doubt he takes comfort that Duke's miserable performance in Seattle fuels the hurricane-causing-butterfly factor that makes the game fun. That doesn't mean we can't, though.

YEAR	TEAM	LVL	AGE	WHIP	ERA	DRA	WARP	MPH	FB%	WHF	CSP
2016	CHA	MLB	33	1.25	2.63	3.92	0.5	92.4	56.9	12.4	45.2
2016	SLN	MLB	33	1.29	1.93	4.65	0.1	92.1	67.4	9.5	48.4
2017	SLN	MLB	34	1.04	3.93	5.47	-0.1	89.7	57.3	13	47.9
2018	MIN	MLB	35	1.58	3.62	3.73	0.5	89.9	47.2	10.9	45.8
2018	SEA	MLB	35	1.30	5.52	3.65	0.2	90.4	53.9	11	43.7
2019	CIN	MLB	36	1.47	4.73	4.67	0.1	89.5	53.1	11.1	45.4

Zach Duke, continued

Pitch Shape vs LHH

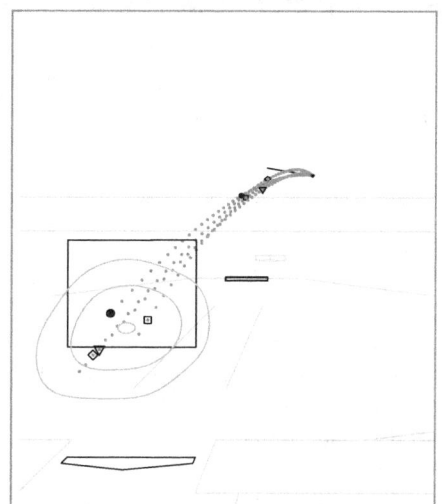

Pitch Shape vs RHH

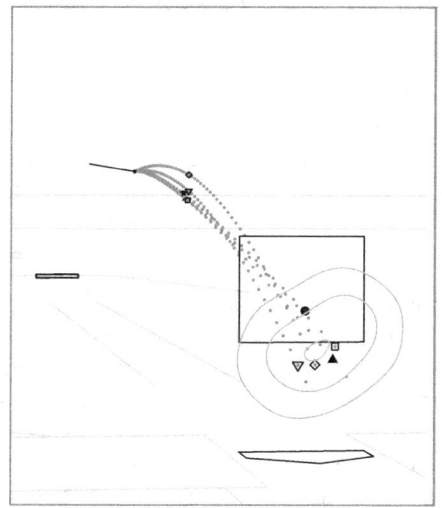

Type	Frequency	Velocity	H Movement	V Movement
● Fastball	9.9%	88.4 [87]	7.3 [97]	-25.8 [68]
☐ Sinker	39.2%	88.9 [82]	12.6 [100]	-30.5 [67]
+ Cutter				
▲ Changeup	12.6%	83.6 [93]	11 [101]	-34.7 [78]
✕ Splitter				
▽ Slider	15.8%	78.4 [73]	-10.4 [124]	-40.4 [78]
◇ Curveball	22.6%	73.7 [83]	-12.3 [119]	-51.9 [91]
⊕ Slow Curveball				
✳ Knuckleball				
▼ Screwball				

Reds Player Analysis - 59

Amir Garrett LHP
Born: 05/03/92   Age: 27   Bats: R   Throws: L
Height: 6'5"   Weight: 228   Origin: Round 22, 2011 Draft (#685 overall)

YEAR	TEAM	LVL	AGE	W	L	SV	G	GS	IP	H	HR	BB/9	K/9	K	GB%	BABIP
2016	PEN	AA	24	5	3	0	13	12	77	51	0	3.3	9.1	78	50%	.252
2016	LOU	AAA	24	2	5	0	12	11	67^2	48	6	4.1	7.2	54	49%	.231
2017	LOU	AAA	25	2	4	0	14	14	67^2	79	7	3.2	8.1	61	41%	.346
2017	CIN	MLB	25	3	8	0	16	14	70^2	74	23	5.1	8.0	63	44%	.264
2018	CIN	MLB	26	1	2	0	66	0	63	56	8	3.6	10.1	71	39%	.306
2019	CIN	MLB	27	2	2	0	46	0	48	40	6	4.1	10.5	57	42%	.288

Breakout: 24%   Improve: 48%   Collapse: 7%   Attrition: 17%   MLB: 66%
Comparables: Billy Buckner, Christian Friedrich, Buck Farmer

Lots of pitching prospects have big fastballs, a bad third pitch and sketchy command, and when they inevitably move to the bullpen it feels like a failure. Not so for Garrett, who embraced his new role wholeheartedly when the Reds sent him to the 'pen last spring after struggling to carve out a niche in the rotation. He found instant success, as his mid-90s fastball played up in shorter stints and he was able to shelve his dodgy changeup and pitch with more emotion. Garrett faded somewhat down the stretch, but his stuff, temperament and experience as a starter make him well-suited to fill the high-leverage, multi-inning relief role all the cool teams have these days.

YEAR	TEAM	LVL	AGE	WHIP	ERA	DRA	WARP	MPH	FB%	WHF	CSP
2016	PEN	AA	24	1.03	1.75	2.95	2.0				
2016	LOU	AAA	24	1.17	3.46	3.90	1.1				
2017	LOU	AAA	25	1.52	5.72	4.57	0.8				
2017	CIN	MLB	25	1.61	7.39	7.46	-1.5	94.4	62.1	9.1	47.7
2018	CIN	MLB	26	1.29	4.29	4.41	0.4	97.1	63.1	14.8	47.5
2019	CIN	MLB	27	1.28	4.06	4.16	0.4	95.3	63.4	12.1	48.1

Amir Garrett, continued

Pitch Shape vs LHH

Pitch Shape vs RHH

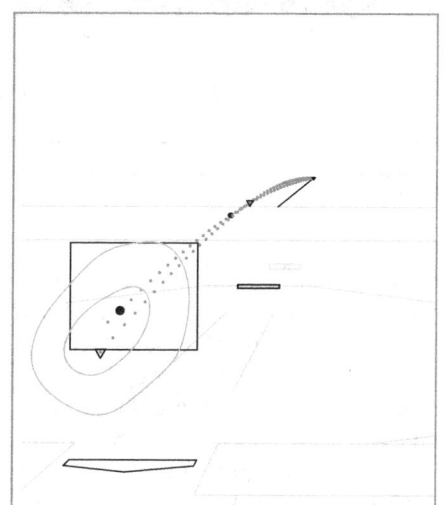
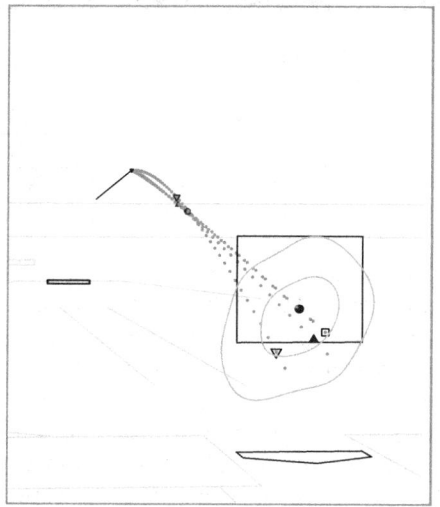

Type	Frequency	Velocity	H Movement	V Movement
● Fastball	54.9%	95.7 [110]	9.9 [85]	-14.4 [104]
☐ Sinker	8.2%	95.5 [115]	13.7 [91]	-17.5 [109]
+ Cutter				
▲ Changeup	3.5%	85.3 [100]	11.6 [98]	-21.9 [116]
✕ Splitter				
▽ Slider	33.4%	84.3 [99]	-0.9 [83]	-32.4 [102]
◇ Curveball				
⊕ Slow Curveball				
✳ Knuckleball				
▼ Screwball				

Cincinnati Reds 2019

Sonny Gray   RHP
Born: 11/07/89   Age: 29   Bats: R   Throws: R
Height: 5'10"   Weight: 190   Origin: Round 1, 2011 Draft (#18 overall)

YEAR	TEAM	LVL	AGE	W	L	SV	G	GS	IP	H	HR	BB/9	K/9	K	GB%	BABIP
2016	OAK	MLB	26	5	11	0	22	22	117	133	18	3.2	7.2	94	54%	.319
2017	OAK	MLB	27	6	5	0	16	16	97	84	8	2.8	8.7	94	58%	.285
2017	NYA	MLB	27	4	7	0	11	11	65[1]	55	11	3.7	8.1	59	48%	.246
2018	NYA	MLB	28	11	9	0	30	23	130[1]	138	14	3.9	8.5	123	52%	.326
2019	CIN	MLB	29	8	8	0	24	24	127	116	15	3.3	8.8	124	51%	.290

Breakout: 12%   Improve: 40%   Collapse: 23%   Attrition: 9%   MLB: 98%
Comparables: Dean Chance, Hyun-jin Ryu, Johnny Cueto

There was once an anonymous Yankees fan who would e-mail every Yankees-affiliated writer, posing as former Yankees to complain about Brian Cashman. It was largely cockamamie, ad hominem gibberish, but inside of almost every e-mail was mention of Cashman's last big flop, Carl Pavano. Even though criticisms have been a bit lighter considering fans got the homegrown "core" they have been clamoring for, one would imagine that a listserv like that today would contain complaints on Sonny Gray, the new teeth-grinder du jour. After being acquired last year for a trio of prospects that likely won't be missed too much, the consensus was that getting Gray was necessary to take them to all the way to the ALCS. Today, many wonder what the world would look like if they had acquired Justin Verlander instead.

YEAR	TEAM	LVL	AGE	WHIP	ERA	DRA	WARP	MPH	FB%	WHF	CSP
2016	OAK	MLB	26	1.50	5.69	4.97	0.5	95.1	64.1	8.8	47.1
2017	OAK	MLB	27	1.18	3.43	4.22	1.5	94.8	63.7	13.1	45.5
2017	NYA	MLB	27	1.26	3.72	4.04	1.1	94.6	63.7	12	41.8
2018	NYA	MLB	28	1.50	4.90	5.00	0.4	95.2	57.2	10.8	45.2
2019	CIN	MLB	29	1.27	4.05	4.10	1.4	94.3	61.1	11.1	45.3

Sonny Gray, continued

Pitch Shape vs LHH

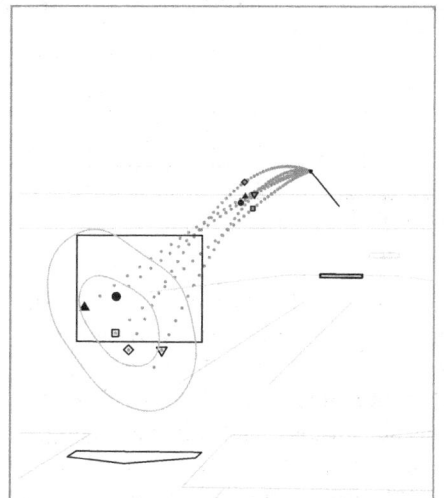

Pitch Shape vs RHH

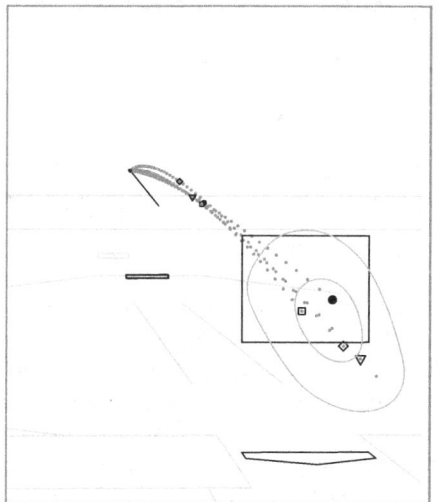

Type	Frequency	Velocity	H Movement	V Movement
● Fastball	25.8%	93.8 [104]	-0.6 [128]	-15.4 [101]
☐ Sinker	29.9%	93.4 [105]	-10.6 [117]	-19.5 [103]
+ Cutter	1.6%	92.1 [120]	2 [101]	-19.3 [118]
▲ Changeup	3.0%	89.6 [117]	-11.6 [98]	-22.5 [114]
✕ Splitter				
▽ Slider	15.9%	85.3 [104]	11.3 [128]	-37.4 [87]
◇ Curveball	23.7%	82.5 [115]	14.6 [129]	-47 [102]
⊕ Slow Curveball	0.2%	76.7 [117]	13.9 [108]	-51.9 [116]
✱ Knuckleball				
▼ Screwball				

David Hernandez   RHP

Born: 05/13/85   Age: 34   Bats: R   Throws: R
Height: 6'3"   Weight: 245   Origin: Round 16, 2005 Draft (#483 overall)

YEAR	TEAM	LVL	AGE	W	L	SV	G	GS	IP	H	HR	BB/9	K/9	K	GB%	BABIP
2016	PHI	MLB	31	3	4	1	70	0	72²	77	11	4.0	9.9	80	40%	.337
2017	GWN	AAA	32	1	0	4	7	0	8	4	0	2.2	10.1	9	44%	.222
2017	ANA	MLB	32	1	0	1	38	0	36¹	29	0	2.0	9.2	37	49%	.309
2017	ARI	MLB	32	2	1	1	26	0	18²	19	4	0.5	7.2	15	36%	.278
2018	CIN	MLB	33	5	2	0	57	0	64	46	6	2.4	9.1	65	34%	.248
2019	*CIN*	*MLB*	*34*	*2*	*3*	*0*	*46*	*0*	*48*	*47*	*8*	*3.5*	*9.3*	*50*	*39%*	*.298*

Breakout: 24%   Improve: 44%   Collapse: 26%   Attrition: 14%   MLB: 86%
Comparables: Will Ohman, Luis Vizcaino, Joe Thatcher

A veteran reliever who has cut down on his walks the last two years, Hernandez must have been extraordinarily nice to Lady Luck to come away with the 1.95 ERA he sported at Great American Ball Park last season given his highest fly-ball rate in five years. His back-of-the-baseball-card stats say that the Reds inking him to a two-year deal last year was a really slick move, while his underlying numbers suggest that it'll be something they end up regretting. The former Oriole, Diamondback, Phillie, Angel and Diamondback once more will slide into a setup role in front of Raisel Iglesias for as long as he can keep the ball out of the stands.

YEAR	TEAM	LVL	AGE	WHIP	ERA	DRA	WARP	MPH	FB%	WHF	CSP
2016	PHI	MLB	31	1.50	3.84	4.47	0.4	96.3	64.3	13.1	49.7
2017	GWN	AAA	32	0.75	1.12	3.39	0.2				
2017	ANA	MLB	32	1.02	2.23	2.56	1.1	95.0	55.1	14.2	49.6
2017	ARI	MLB	32	1.07	4.82	3.80	0.3	95.0	55.1	12.4	49.4
2018	CIN	MLB	33	0.98	2.53	4.71	0.2	94.5	58.3	12.2	49.3
2019	*CIN*	*MLB*	*34*	*1.37*	*4.91*	*4.81*	*0.0*	*94.0*	*58.4*	*12.7*	*48.7*

David Hernandez, continued

Pitch Shape vs LHH

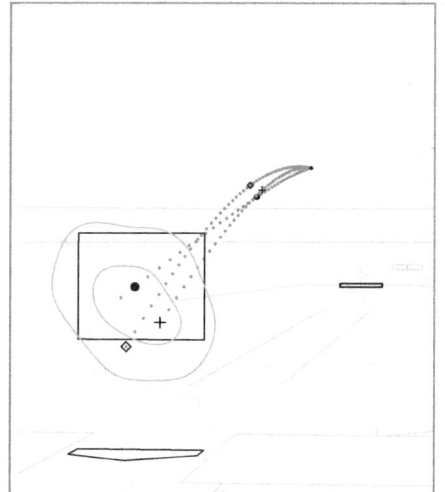

Pitch Shape vs RHH

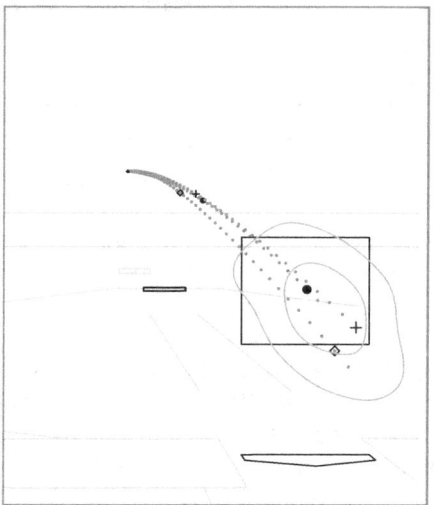

Type	Frequency	Velocity	H Movement	V Movement
● Fastball	58.3%	93.6 [103]	-11.2 [79]	-15.9 [100]
☐ Sinker				
+ Cutter	19.0%	86.2 [85]	2.8 [106]	-28.7 [80]
▲ Changeup	3.0%	87.8 [110]	-8.3 [116]	-23.6 [111]
✕ Splitter				
▽ Slider				
◇ Curveball	19.8%	81.5 [111]	10.1 [110]	-36.7 [126]
✥ Slow Curveball				
✱ Knuckleball				
▼ Screwball				

Jared Hughes   RHP

Born: 07/04/85   Age: 33   Bats: R   Throws: R
Height: 6'7"   Weight: 240   Origin: Round 4, 2006 Draft (#110 overall)

YEAR	TEAM	LVL	AGE	W	L	SV	G	GS	IP	H	HR	BB/9	K/9	K	GB%	BABIP
2016	PIT	MLB	30	1	1	1	67	0	59^1	62	6	3.3	5.2	34	59%	.295
2017	MIL	MLB	31	5	3	1	67	0	59^2	49	4	3.6	7.2	48	63%	.278
2018	CIN	MLB	32	4	3	7	72	0	78^2	57	4	2.6	6.8	59	66%	.252
2019	CIN	MLB	33	2	2	4	46	0	48	45	5	3.9	7.6	41	58%	.290

Breakout: 27%   Improve: 43%   Collapse: 22%   Attrition: 8%   MLB: 82%
Comparables: Brad Ziegler, Jim Johnson, Kent Tekulve

Hughes doesn't strike out a lot of batters, but despite recent MLB trends, he's never had to in order to be effective. Another top-five ground-ball rate among relievers due to his heavy sinker use certainly helps. You can argue that his BABIP isn't sustainable, especially when he keeps the ball on the ground at such an extreme clip, but a career .275 BABIP is indicative of an arm batters just don't square up well. What's more, he had the best swinging strike rate of his career in 2018, but don't expect it to lead to an uptick in strikeouts as it came with an equal but opposite decrease in velocity. A veteran reliever who can go more than one inning when asked and dominates in save situations—Hughes had a pristine 1.03 ERA under such circumstances—is a valuable commodity for any team.

YEAR	TEAM	LVL	AGE	WHIP	ERA	DRA	WARP	MPH	FB%	WHF	CSP
2016	PIT	MLB	30	1.42	3.03	6.40	-1.0	95.6	81.8	10.3	39.2
2017	MIL	MLB	31	1.22	3.02	5.86	-0.5	95.1	77.4	12.5	41.9
2018	CIN	MLB	32	1.02	1.94	4.59	0.3	93.4	86	12.8	42.2
2019	CIN	MLB	33	1.35	4.35	4.37	0.2	93.3	81.4	12	40.9

Jared Hughes, continued

Pitch Shape vs LHH

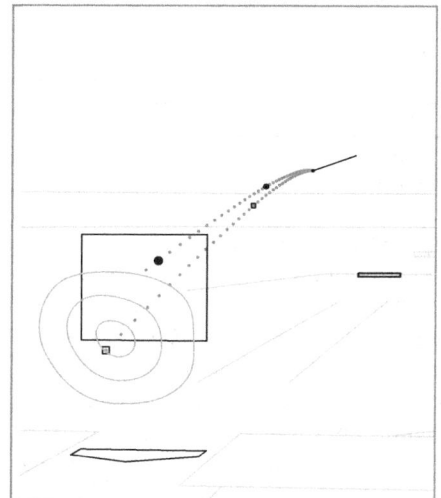

Pitch Shape vs RHH

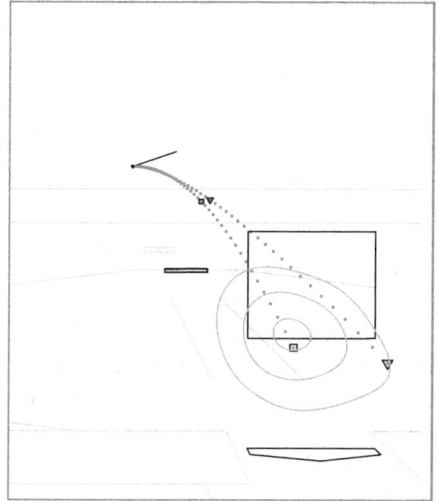

Type	Frequency	Velocity	H Movement	V Movement
● Fastball	8.5%	93.4 [103]	-10.7 [81]	-19.2 [89]
☐ Sinker	77.5%	92.3 [99]	-13.6 [92]	-30.2 [68]
+ Cutter				
▲ Changeup	0.8%	88.5 [113]	-12.6 [93]	-31.5 [88]
✕ Splitter				
▽ Slider	13.3%	86.3 [108]	3 [92]	-30.7 [107]
◇ Curveball				
⊕ Slow Curveball				
✻ Knuckleball				
▼ Screwball				

Raisel Iglesias   RHP
Born: 01/04/90   Age: 29   Bats: R   Throws: R
Height: 6'2"   Weight: 188   Origin: International Free Agent, 2014

YEAR	TEAM	LVL	AGE	W	L	SV	G	GS	IP	H	HR	BB/9	K/9	K	GB%	BABIP
2016	CIN	MLB	26	3	2	6	37	5	78¹	63	7	3.0	9.5	83	43%	.275
2017	CIN	MLB	27	3	3	28	63	0	76	57	5	3.2	10.9	92	43%	.287
2018	CIN	MLB	28	2	5	30	66	0	72	52	12	3.1	10.0	80	40%	.233
2019	CIN	MLB	29	3	3	31	51	0	53	44	6	3.5	10.5	63	41%	.285

Breakout: 15%   Improve: 42%   Collapse: 26%   Attrition: 9%   MLB: 98%
Comparables: Ramon Ramirez, Frank Francisco, Scott Linebrink

Another flame-throwing Cuban the Reds hoped would find success in the rotation, but instead has bowled over hitters out of the bullpen. Iglesias doesn't have the 100-mph fastball of Aroldis Chapman, but it's hard to quibble with the intensely consistent results from his three seasons in the Queen City. Yet despite the consistency, two things set Iglesias' season apart from the prior two: his touch of gopheritis and the development of his cambio. After allowing only 12 homers in his first two seasons, he matched that number in 2018—with most of the damage coming off his fastball. A relatively stable batted ball profile implies that this is a one-year blip. On the other side, he threw his changeup nearly twice as often last season, helping him narrow what was a 200-plus point platoon split differential to almost even. In fact, he pulled that string 231 times last season against left-handed hitters and allowed only one extra-base hit—a double to Colin Moran on the last day of the season. As reliable as a 3-Way at Skyline, Iglesias will again be the glue that holds together the Reds bullpen in 2019.

YEAR	TEAM	LVL	AGE	WHIP	ERA	DRA	WARP	MPH	FB%	WHF	CSP
2016	CIN	MLB	26	1.14	2.53	3.32	1.6	97.9	54.6	12.9	49.1
2017	CIN	MLB	27	1.11	2.49	3.34	1.6	98.6	57.1	15.1	50.2
2018	CIN	MLB	28	1.07	2.38	3.48	1.2	97.7	50.2	16.5	47.9
2019	CIN	MLB	29	1.19	3.43	3.64	0.7	97.4	53.7	15.1	49

Raisel Iglesias, continued

Pitch Shape vs LHH

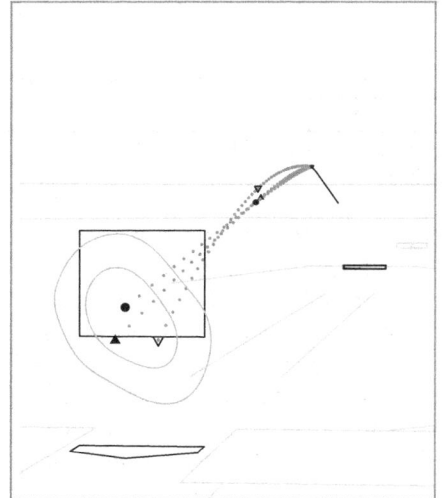

Pitch Shape vs RHH

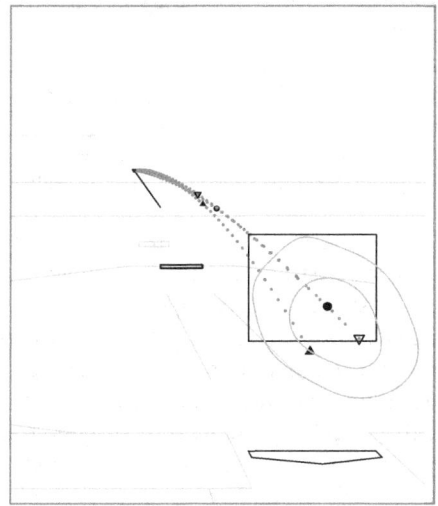

Type		Frequency	Velocity	H Movement	V Movement
●	Fastball	49.9%	95.8 [111]	-11.1 [79]	-15.2 [102]
□	Sinker	0.3%	89.8 [87]	-15.4 [77]	-25.3 [84]
+	Cutter				
▲	Changeup	23.4%	88.3 [112]	-14.1 [85]	-27.6 [99]
×	Splitter				
▽	Slider	26.4%	85.5 [105]	7.5 [111]	-32.5 [101]
◇	Curveball				
⊕	Slow Curveball				
✳	Knuckleball				
▼	Screwball				

Michael Lorenzen   RHP

Born: 01/04/92   Age: 27   Bats: R   Throws: R
Height: 6'3"   Weight: 217   Origin: Round 1, 2013 Draft (#38 overall)

YEAR	TEAM	LVL	AGE	W	L	SV	G	GS	IP	H	HR	BB/9	K/9	K	GB%	BABIP
2016	CIN	MLB	24	2	1	0	35	0	50	41	5	2.3	8.6	48	64%	.277
2017	CIN	MLB	25	8	4	2	70	0	83	78	9	3.7	8.7	80	57%	.295
2018	CIN	MLB	26	4	2	1	45	3	81	78	6	3.8	6.0	54	52%	.291
2019	CIN	MLB	27	3	3	0	49	3	64^1	63	8	3.9	7.9	56	53%	.296

Breakout: 19%   Improve: 36%   Collapse: 21%   Attrition: 13%   MLB: 80%
Comparables: Erasmo Ramirez, Noah Lowry, Andrew Cashner

Lorenzen isn't the most dominant of multi-inning relievers, but he may be the most interesting. He throws hard yet doesn't miss bats, relying on his mid-90s power sinker and worm-killing cutter to keep the ball in the yard and runs off the scoreboard. He has real skill at the plate, not "careful, he has some power" skill but "start him off with a breaking ball and then work the edges" skill. And his ability to move a full glass of water balanced on his forehead to the floor without spilling, involving a squat, a back roll and a two-knee pinch, belongs in the Stupid Human Tricks Hall of Fame (seriously, go watch that). The Reds have said they're open to him starting or relieving or even playing the outfield on occasion to get his bat in the lineup and save a roster spot. We love this, of course, but not as much as we love the idea of pairing Lorenzen with Amir Garrett as an athletic, lefty-righty, pitcher-outfield tandem, swapping them back and forth based on batter handedness. Betcha the Rays would do it.

YEAR	TEAM	LVL	AGE	WHIP	ERA	DRA	WARP	MPH	FB%	WHF	CSP
2016	CIN	MLB	24	1.08	2.88	3.61	0.8	98.6	47.8	10.5	47.4
2017	CIN	MLB	25	1.35	4.45	4.37	0.7	97.9	51.3	11.3	47.8
2018	CIN	MLB	26	1.38	3.11	5.87	-0.8	96.9	51.5	7.6	48.6
2019	CIN	MLB	27	1.42	4.69	4.65	0.2	97.1	51.5	9.6	48.6

Michael Lorenzen, continued

Pitch Shape vs LHH

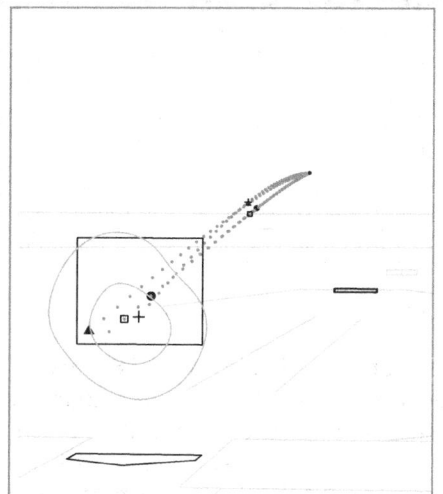

Pitch Shape vs RHH

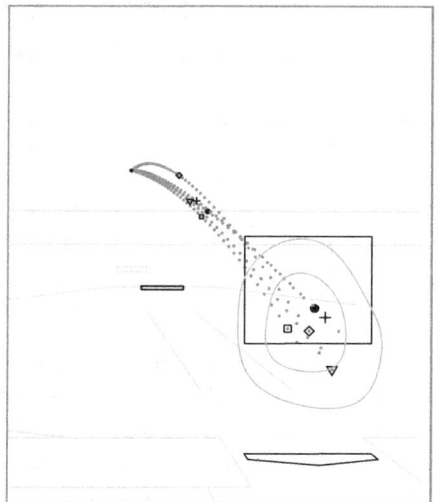

Type	Frequency	Velocity	H Movement	V Movement
● Fastball	10.7%	96.1 [111]	-7.8 [95]	-12.6 [110]
☐ Sinker	40.8%	95.4 [115]	-12 [105]	-16.1 [114]
+ Cutter	30.3%	90.9 [113]	2.7 [105]	-23.7 [100]
▲ Changeup	7.4%	87.7 [110]	-10.9 [102]	-22.7 [114]
✕ Splitter				
▽ Slider	6.2%	86 [107]	3.4 [93]	-34.6 [95]
◇ Curveball	4.6%	82.2 [114]	5.5 [90]	-48.3 [99]
⊕ Slow Curveball				
✳ Knuckleball				
▼ Screwball				

Tyler Mahle RHP
Born: 09/29/94   Age: 24   Bats: R   Throws: R
Height: 6'3"   Weight: 210   Origin: Round 7, 2013 Draft (#225 overall)

YEAR	TEAM	LVL	AGE	W	L	SV	G	GS	IP	H	HR	BB/9	K/9	K	GB%	BABIP
2016	DAY	A+	21	8	3	0	13	13	79¹	58	6	1.9	8.6	76	48%	.255
2016	PEN	AA	21	6	3	0	14	14	71¹	78	12	2.5	8.2	65	42%	.320
2017	PEN	AA	22	7	3	0	14	14	85	57	5	1.8	9.2	87	42%	.245
2017	LOU	AAA	22	3	4	0	10	10	59¹	52	4	2.0	7.7	51	42%	.281
2017	CIN	MLB	22	1	2	0	4	4	20	19	0	4.9	6.3	14	56%	.302
2018	LOU	AAA	23	2	1	0	5	5	29²	22	4	3.3	6.1	20	39%	.209
2018	CIN	MLB	23	7	9	0	23	23	112	125	22	4.3	8.8	110	41%	.324
2019	CIN	MLB	24	6	6	0	18	18	95	89	14	3.3	8.9	95	41%	.292

Breakout: 19%   Improve: 43%   Collapse: 12%   Attrition: 25%   MLB: 72%
Comparables: Reynaldo Lopez, Daniel Mengden, Robbie Ray

"The lack of a special fastball could result in a bunch of homers at GABP," we said in our 2018 Cincinnati Top 10 Prospects article. Nailed it. Of the 22 long balls that helped torpedo Mahle's rookie season, 17 were launched at home. In related news, lefties took Mahle deep 15 times as part of the .300/.414/.576 hurtin' they laid on him. His low-90s heater and solid slider can miss bats, but spectral command and an inconsistent changeup produce too many walks and meatballs over the plate. None of this is to say Mahle isn't worth another look, but the young Californian will need to find a way to make hitters less comfortable if he wants to stick in a big-league rotation.

YEAR	TEAM	LVL	AGE	WHIP	ERA	DRA	WARP	MPH	FB%	WHF	CSP
2016	DAY	A+	21	0.95	2.50	3.44	1.8				
2016	PEN	AA	21	1.37	4.92	3.04	1.8				
2017	PEN	AA	22	0.87	1.59	3.12	2.1				
2017	LOU	AAA	22	1.10	2.73	4.66	0.7				
2017	CIN	MLB	22	1.50	2.70	5.48	0.0	95.5	65.8	7.9	47.2
2018	LOU	AAA	23	1.11	2.73	8.09	-0.8				
2018	CIN	MLB	23	1.59	4.98	6.30	-1.3	95.4	67.8	11.4	49.6
2019	CIN	MLB	24	1.29	4.34	4.41	0.7	95.2	69.6	11.3	50

Tyler Mahle, continued

Pitch Shape vs LHH

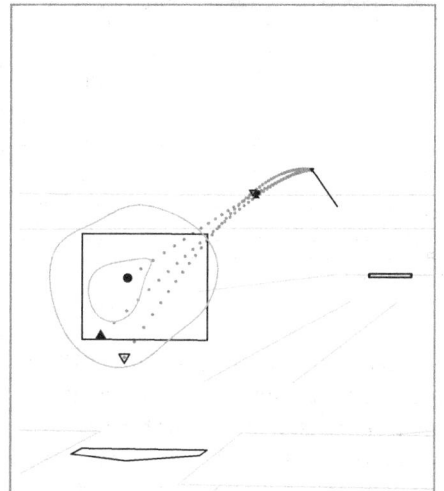

Pitch Shape vs RHH

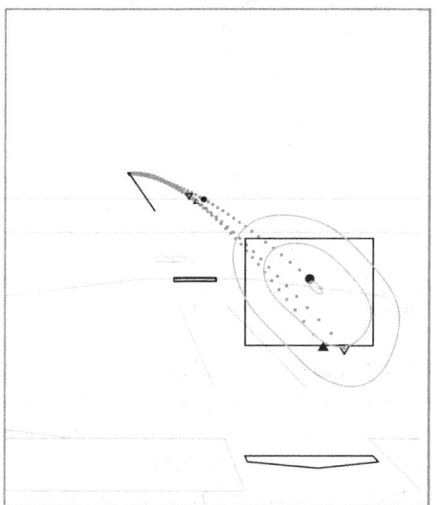

Type	Frequency	Velocity	H Movement	V Movement
● Fastball	67.8%	93.1 [102]	-9.6 [86]	-14.9 [103]
☐ Sinker				
+ Cutter	0.6%	86.7 [88]	0.3 [91]	-25.3 [94]
▲ Changeup	11.3%	84.1 [95]	-9.6 [109]	-26.5 [102]
× Splitter				
▽ Slider	19.7%	83.9 [97]	4.7 [99]	-34.3 [96]
◇ Curveball	0.6%	77.9 [98]	8.1 [101]	-41.7 [114]
⊕ Slow Curveball				
✳ Knuckleball				
▼ Screwball				

Keury Mella RHP

Born: 08/02/93   Age: 25   Bats: R   Throws: R
Height: 6'2"   Weight: 200   Origin: International Free Agent, 2012

YEAR	TEAM	LVL	AGE	W	L	SV	G	GS	IP	H	HR	BB/9	K/9	K	GB%	BABIP
2016	DAY	A+	22	8	9	0	25	24	131^2	150	7	3.8	6.5	95	47%	.340
2016	LOU	AAA	22	1	0	0	1	1	7	3	1	1.3	7.7	6	65%	.125
2017	PEN	AA	23	4	10	1	27	26	134	135	14	2.9	7.3	109	47%	.300
2017	CIN	MLB	23	0	0	0	2	0	4	5	1	4.5	2.2	1	31%	.267
2018	PEN	AA	24	7	3	0	16	16	85	70	8	3.3	9.2	87	49%	.276
2018	CIN	MLB	24	0	0	0	4	0	9^1	13	4	7.7	7.7	8	36%	.333
2018	LOU	AAA	24	2	1	0	5	5	23	20	1	2.3	5.5	14	42%	.271
2019	CIN	MLB	25	2	2	0	15	5	35	37	5	4.1	8.1	32	44%	.298

Breakout: 9%   Improve: 15%   Collapse: 8%   Attrition: 19%   MLB: 27%
Comparables: Cesar Valdez, Thad Weber, Graham Godfrey

Mella has taken steps forward for each of his seasons with the Reds. In 2017 he improved his strikeouts and walks while moving up to Double-A, and when he repeated that level in 2018, he missed even more bats. If Mella wants to be taken seriously as a member of the Reds bullpen in 2019, he'll need to work on getting batters to chase more out of the zone. Like seemingly everyone else who tried to pitch for the Reds last season, his tiny MLB sample in 2018 was one to forget. Of course, the 25-year-old still holds out some hope of being able to start as well, but one-pitch starters aren't the most successful breed.

YEAR	TEAM	LVL	AGE	WHIP	ERA	DRA	WARP	MPH	FB%	WHF	CSP
2016	DAY	A+	22	1.56	3.90	6.32	-1.3				
2016	LOU	AAA	22	0.57	1.29	5.60	0.0				
2017	PEN	AA	23	1.33	4.30	3.68	2.4				
2017	CIN	MLB	23	1.75	6.75	8.01	-0.1	97.4	72.7	3.6	60.1
2018	PEN	AA	24	1.19	3.07	4.27	1.1				
2018	CIN	MLB	24	2.25	8.68	9.04	-0.4	96.7	70.8	9.4	51
2018	LOU	AAA	24	1.13	2.74	6.04	-0.1				
2019	CIN	MLB	25	1.48	5.03	5.02	0.0	96.6	72.8	8.6	56.4

Keury Mella, continued

Pitch Shape vs LHH

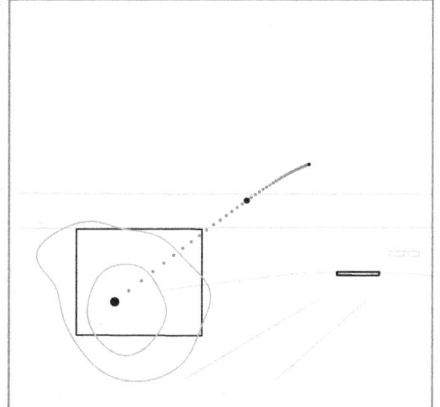

Pitch Shape vs RHH

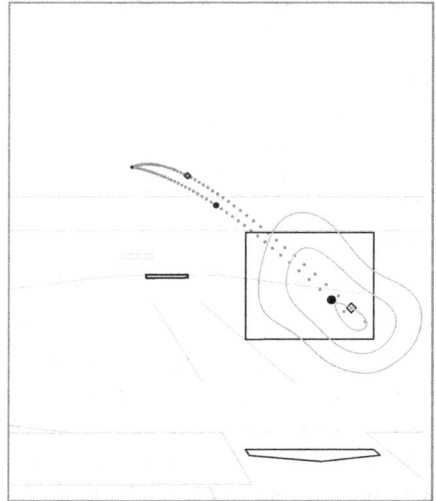

Type	Frequency	Velocity	H Movement	V Movement
● Fastball	70.8%	94.8 [107]	-9.1 [89]	-14.5 [104]
☐ Sinker				
+ Cutter				
▲ Changeup	10.9%	83.3 [92]	-12.7 [93]	-29.4 [94]
× Splitter				
▽ Slider				
◇ Curveball	18.3%	80.3 [107]	7.5 [99]	-36.3 [127]
✦ Slow Curveball				
✻ Knuckleball				
▼ Screwball				

Wandy Peralta   LHP

Born: 07/27/91   Age: 27   Bats: L   Throws: L
Height: 6'0"   Weight: 220   Origin: International Free Agent, 2009

YEAR	TEAM	LVL	AGE	W	L	SV	G	GS	IP	H	HR	BB/9	K/9	K	GB%	BABIP
2016	PEN	AA	24	0	1	0	13	0	17^2	17	1	1.5	10.2	20	50%	.327
2016	LOU	AAA	24	4	1	3	37	2	58	44	2	3.6	5.9	38	61%	.249
2016	CIN	MLB	24	0	0	0	10	0	7^1	11	1	8.6	6.1	5	46%	.400
2017	CIN	MLB	25	3	4	0	69	0	64^2	53	8	3.3	7.9	57	56%	.260
2018	LOU	AAA	26	1	0	0	13	0	14^1	13	1	4.4	6.3	10	57%	.293
2018	CIN	MLB	26	2	2	0	59	0	45^1	58	2	6.2	6.2	31	48%	.348
2019	CIN	MLB	27	2	2	0	41	0	43	43	6	4.6	8.0	38	50%	.299

Breakout: 22%   Improve: 41%   Collapse: 16%   Attrition: 19%   MLB: 70%
Comparables: Ryan Pressly, Chris Bassitt, Logan Ondrusek

There's a lovely symmetry that goes along with finishing a season with the same number of both walks and strikeouts. If you're a hitter. In Peralta's case, it was a not-so-slow descent into accommodating the next wave of failing Reds' arms, as the southpaw took a step back in every facet of his performance. There's a slight glimmer of hope because he was better after he returned from his minor league demotion, but even an ERA around 4 and a middling strikeout rate isn't enough to lock him into a regular role on the 25-man roster.

YEAR	TEAM	LVL	AGE	WHIP	ERA	DRA	WARP	MPH	FB%	WHF	CSP
2016	PEN	AA	24	1.13	3.06	3.07	0.4				
2016	LOU	AAA	24	1.16	2.33	3.42	1.1				
2016	CIN	MLB	24	2.45	8.59	8.69	-0.3	97.5	62.9	14.4	44.5
2017	CIN	MLB	25	1.19	3.76	4.38	0.6	98.0	53.3	15.5	45.2
2018	LOU	AAA	26	1.40	3.14	3.75	0.2				
2018	CIN	MLB	26	1.96	5.36	7.53	-1.4	97.1	48.8	10.7	48.2
2019	CIN	MLB	27	1.52	5.20	5.01	-0.1	97.1	52.1	13.3	46.8

Wandy Peralta, continued

Pitch Shape vs LHH

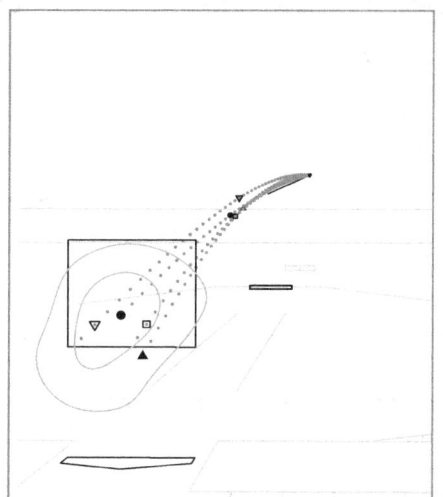

Pitch Shape vs RHH

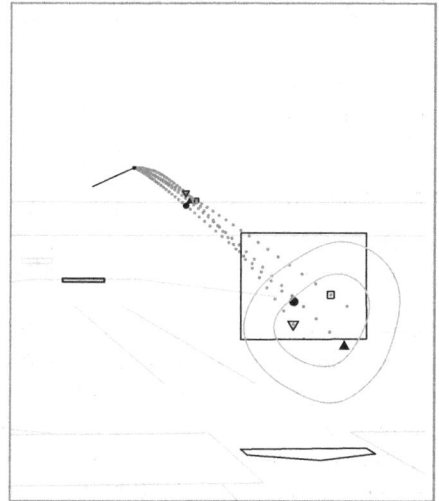

Type	Frequency	Velocity	H Movement	V Movement
● Fastball	24.9%	96.3 [112]	9.2 [88]	-14 [105]
□ Sinker	23.9%	95.8 [117]	14.1 [87]	-17.5 [109]
+ Cutter				
▲ Changeup	30.6%	87.8 [110]	14.1 [85]	-27.1 [101]
× Splitter				
▽ Slider	20.6%	87.2 [112]	0.4 [77]	-29.4 [111]
◇ Curveball				
⊕ Slow Curveball				
✳ Knuckleball				
▼ Screwball				

Cody Reed   LHP

Born: 04/15/93   Age: 26   Bats: L   Throws: L
Height: 6'5"   Weight: 230   Origin: Round 2, 2013 Draft (#46 overall)

YEAR	TEAM	LVL	AGE	W	L	SV	G	GS	IP	H	HR	BB/9	K/9	K	GB%	BABIP
2016	CIN	MLB	23	0	7	0	10	10	47^2	67	12	3.6	8.1	43	54%	.364
2016	LOU	AAA	23	6	4	0	13	13	73	71	6	2.5	8.0	65	52%	.314
2017	LOU	AAA	24	4	9	0	21	20	106^1	105	7	5.2	8.6	102	50%	.328
2017	CIN	MLB	24	1	1	1	12	1	17^2	11	3	9.7	8.7	17	65%	.200
2018	LOU	AAA	25	4	8	0	18	17	105^2	109	13	2.6	8.9	105	46%	.325
2018	CIN	MLB	25	1	3	0	17	7	43	45	5	3.1	8.8	42	63%	.323
2019	CIN	MLB	26	2	2	0	15	5	35	35	5	3.8	9.0	36	49%	.302

Breakout: 23%   Improve: 45%   Collapse: 21%   Attrition: 38%   MLB: 76%
Comparables: J.R. Graham, Joe Saunders, Allen Webster

It's been a couple of long years since Reed was the centerpiece in the deadline deal that sent Johnny Cueto to Kansas City. Hyped as a potential no. 3 starter with a plus-plus slider, Reed has been tattooed in 18 career starts for the Reds, giving up a .315/.387/.537 slash line and making him persona non grata when the team was given any other options. The slider was basically the pitch that was promised in 2018—he threw it over 40 percent of the time and allowed a .268 slugging percentage. Unfortunately, when you transform into a sinker/slider pitcher, it also implies that you throw a sinker. When Reed keeps the pitch down, it can work, but it didn't happen nearly enough and righties tore through the ticked-down version. The southpaw is now out of options and is likely to once again fill a swing role, but without improved command or rediscovered velocity, his days of starting are likely over.

YEAR	TEAM	LVL	AGE	WHIP	ERA	DRA	WARP	MPH	FB%	WHF	CSP
2016	CIN	MLB	23	1.80	7.36	5.26	0.1	95.8	52.7	10.4	45.7
2016	LOU	AAA	23	1.25	3.08	3.41	1.6				
2017	LOU	AAA	24	1.56	3.55	4.84	1.0				
2017	CIN	MLB	24	1.70	5.09	4.82	0.1	96.2	51.2	13.9	40.4
2018	LOU	AAA	25	1.32	3.92	3.66	2.2				
2018	CIN	MLB	25	1.40	3.98	4.36	0.4	94.9	50.2	11	48.1
2019	CIN	MLB	26	1.42	4.28	4.33	0.3	95.0	52.2	11.5	45.7

Cody Reed, continued

Pitch Shape vs LHH

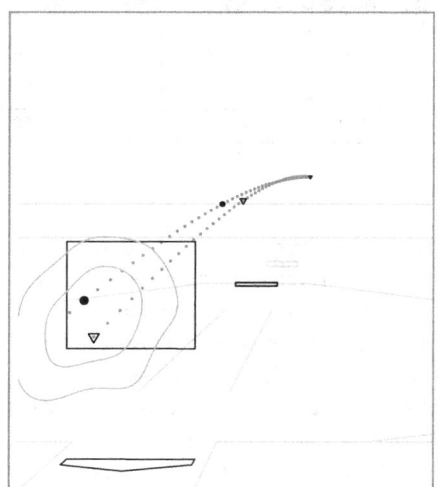

Pitch Shape vs RHH

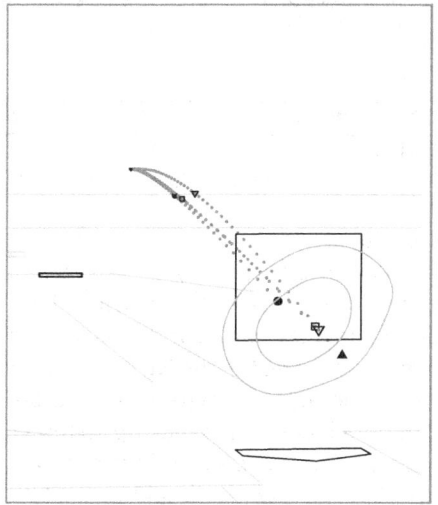

Type	Frequency	Velocity	H Movement	V Movement
● Fastball	22.1%	93.2 [102]	7.1 [98]	-20 [86]
☐ Sinker	28.1%	92.6 [100]	14 [88]	-27.2 [78]
+ Cutter				
▲ Changeup	9.2%	87 [107]	13.5 [88]	-28.6 [96]
✕ Splitter				
▽ Slider	40.6%	87.3 [112]	-3.3 [93]	-31.6 [104]
◇ Curveball				
✦ Slow Curveball				
✳ Knuckleball				
▼ Screwball				

Reds Player Analysis - 79

Tanner Roark RHP

Born: 10/05/86 Age: 32 Bats: R Throws: R
Height: 6'2" Weight: 229 Origin: Round 25, 2008 Draft (#753 overall)

YEAR	TEAM	LVL	AGE	W	L	SV	G	GS	IP	H	HR	BB/9	K/9	K	GB%	BABIP
2016	WAS	MLB	29	16	10	0	34	33	210	173	17	3.1	7.4	172	51%	.269
2017	WAS	MLB	30	13	11	0	32	30	181^1	178	23	3.2	8.2	166	49%	.300
2018	WAS	MLB	31	9	15	0	31	30	180^1	181	24	2.5	7.3	146	43%	.296
2019	CIN	MLB	32	10	9	0	26	26	156	149	24	3.0	8.1	141	46%	.288

Breakout: 10%   Improve: 38%   Collapse: 34%   Attrition: 14%   MLB: 93%
Comparables: Clay Buchholz, Doug Fister, Kevin Millwood

Roark did a new thing in 2018, which will catch your eye given his steady tendencies. Don't worry, you still need an electron microscope to detect pitch-mix changes, a pair of special jewelers' glasses to inspect variations in his peripheral numbers. But the naked eye will show, until the heat death of the internet, that he led the NL in losses last season. Roark has long been a contemporary prototype for that less-than-desirable black ink. Terrible pitchers don't pitch enough to rack up 15 losses. Very, very average pitchers, on the other hand, can go six innings per start, start 30 times in a season and post mid-4.00 ERAs while remaining useful to their teams but catching exactly the wrong wave of results. May Roark wear it as a badge of honor, now in Cincinnati.

YEAR	TEAM	LVL	AGE	WHIP	ERA	DRA	WARP	MPH	FB%	WHF	CSP
2016	WAS	MLB	29	1.17	2.83	3.85	3.6	94.7	62.4	9.6	45.2
2017	WAS	MLB	30	1.33	4.67	3.89	3.4	94.3	56.2	10.7	45.3
2018	WAS	MLB	31	1.28	4.34	4.89	0.9	93.3	59.2	9.2	46.9
2019	CIN	MLB	32	1.28	4.52	4.60	0.8	93.1	58.5	9.7	45.5

Tanner Roark, continued

Pitch Shape vs LHH

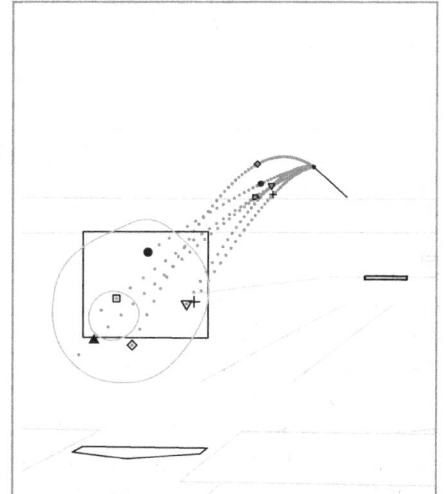

Pitch Shape vs RHH

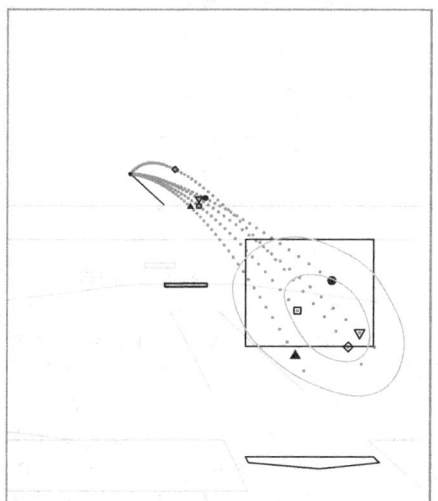

Type		Frequency	Velocity	H Movement	V Movement
●	Fastball	19.2%	91.9 [98]	-5.6 [105]	-14.1 [105]
☐	Sinker	40.0%	91.7 [96]	-11.8 [107]	-17.4 [110]
+	Cutter	2.2%	89.5 [105]	1 [95]	-19.1 [119]
▲	Changeup	12.1%	83.8 [94]	-11.7 [98]	-25.6 [105]
✕	Splitter				
▽	Slider	12.5%	85.3 [104]	3.6 [95]	-27.8 [115]
◇	Curveball	14.0%	75.1 [87]	12.2 [118]	-57.3 [79]
✦	Slow Curveball				
✳	Knuckleball				
▼	Screwball				

Sal Romano   RHP

Born: 10/12/93   Age: 25   Bats: L   Throws: R
Height: 6'5"   Weight: 270   Origin: Round 23, 2011 Draft (#715 overall)

YEAR	TEAM	LVL	AGE	W	L	SV	G	GS	IP	H	HR	BB/9	K/9	K	GB%	BABIP
2016	PEN	AA	22	6	11	0	27	27	156	157	10	2.0	8.3	144	49%	.320
2017	LOU	AAA	23	1	4	0	10	10	49^1	49	1	3.1	5.8	32	50%	.298
2017	CIN	MLB	23	5	8	0	16	16	87	91	9	3.8	7.6	73	53%	.314
2018	CIN	MLB	24	8	11	0	39	25	145^2	155	23	3.3	6.5	105	47%	.288
2019	CIN	MLB	25	2	2	0	31	0	32^1	32	4	3.4	8.3	30	47%	.299

Breakout: 24%   Improve: 54%   Collapse: 23%   Attrition: 36%   MLB: 93%
Comparables: Mike Foltynewicz, Ricky Nolasco, Jeff Hoffman

How acute were the Reds gopher ball woes last year? Of the six Whiplash Brigade members who worked at least 100 innings, Romano's rate of 1.4 home runs per nine innings was the best, yet still ranked as the 13th worst in the National League. Ye gods. Yet there's definitely hope for Romano, a massive right-hander with two bona fide big-league pitches: a slider and a mid-90s sinker that generates plenty of ground ball outs. He tinkered with a cutter last year but doesn't seem to trust it and his changeup is pretty much vaporware, so lefties sprinted to the plate to face him and posted a .303/.373/.528 line. If he can't get that sorted out soon, he'll be bullpen bound.

YEAR	TEAM	LVL	AGE	WHIP	ERA	DRA	WARP	MPH	FB%	WHF	CSP
2016	PEN	AA	22	1.22	3.52	2.65	4.6				
2017	LOU	AAA	23	1.34	3.47	5.51	0.1				
2017	CIN	MLB	23	1.47	4.45	4.55	1.0	97.1	62.7	9.6	46.6
2018	CIN	MLB	24	1.43	5.31	5.76	-0.8	95.8	65.6	8.6	49.1
2019	CIN	MLB	25	1.37	4.19	4.25	0.2	95.9	66.1	9.2	49.1

Sal Romano, continued

Pitch Shape vs LHH

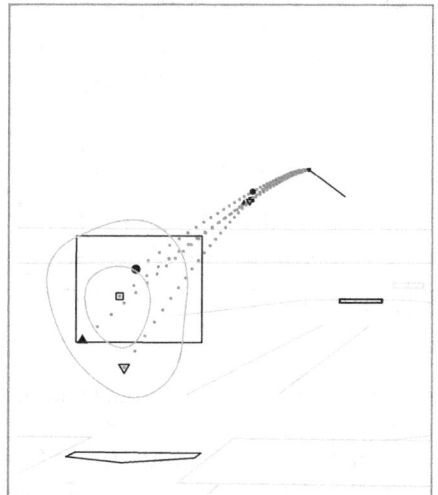

Pitch Shape vs RHH

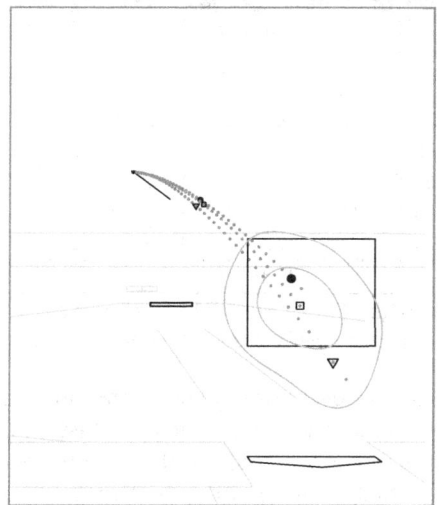

Type	Frequency	Velocity	H Movement	V Movement
● Fastball	4.9%	95.1 [108]	-7.1 [98]	-14.5 [104]
☐ Sinker	60.6%	94.7 [111]	-11.6 [108]	-16.6 [112]
+ Cutter	1.2%	89 [101]	1.8 [99]	-27.4 [85]
▲ Changeup	5.3%	88.2 [112]	-8.6 [114]	-23 [113]
× Splitter				
▽ Slider	28.0%	87.2 [112]	2.2 [88]	-31.3 [105]
◇ Curveball				
⊕ Slow Curveball				
✳ Knuckleball				
▼ Screwball				

Lucas Sims RHP

Born: 05/10/94   Age: 25   Bats: R   Throws: R
Height: 6'2"   Weight: 230   Origin: Round 1, 2012 Draft (#21 overall)

YEAR	TEAM	LVL	AGE	W	L	SV	G	GS	IP	H	HR	BB/9	K/9	K	GB%	BABIP
2016	GWN	AAA	22	2	6	0	11	10	50	56	12	6.7	10.4	58	42%	.333
2016	MIS	AA	22	5	5	0	17	17	91	64	3	5.4	10.0	101	42%	.276
2017	GWN	AAA	23	7	4	0	20	19	115[1]	95	19	2.8	10.3	132	35%	.275
2017	ATL	MLB	23	3	6	0	14	10	57[2]	64	9	3.6	6.9	44	40%	.314
2018	ATL	MLB	24	0	0	0	6	0	10[1]	12	2	7.0	8.7	10	42%	.323
2018	GWN	AAA	24	4	3	0	15	14	73	66	6	4.2	10.2	83	44%	.330
2018	LOU	AAA	24	0	2	0	5	5	28[1]	20	5	1.6	10.2	32	29%	.224
2018	CIN	MLB	24	0	0	0	3	0	5[1]	3	1	8.4	10.1	6	23%	.167
2019	CIN	MLB	25	2	2	0	15	5	35	32	5	4.6	9.9	39	39%	.294

Breakout: 16%   Improve: 34%   Collapse: 23%   Attrition: 43%   MLB: 71%
Comparables: Fabio Castro, Aaron Blair, Keyvius Sampson

Being traded from the organization whose prospect lists you once graced highly to one with which you have no history is freeing if you've yet to establish yourself as a notable contributor to date. It's akin to a celebrity putting on a fake mustache and roaming the streets of Los Angeles just doing things normal people do, like grabbing a double-double at In-N-Out or taking in a matinee at Century City. Sims celebrated that freedom by doing some walking of his own. The Georgia native certainly meshes well with his new team by simply being a formerly famous starting pitching prospect with little to no control, but just because you can fit in doesn't mean you should.

YEAR	TEAM	LVL	AGE	WHIP	ERA	DRA	WARP	MPH	FB%	WHF	CSP
2016	GWN	AAA	22	1.86	7.56	3.97	0.8				
2016	MIS	AA	22	1.31	2.67	3.11	2.2				
2017	GWN	AAA	23	1.14	3.75	3.67	2.5				
2017	ATL	MLB	23	1.51	5.62	6.13	-0.4	93.8	46.5	9	46.7
2018	ATL	MLB	24	1.94	7.84	6.38	-0.2	94.8	55	10	37.4
2018	GWN	AAA	24	1.37	2.84	4.83	0.6				
2018	LOU	AAA	24	0.88	3.81	3.84	0.5				
2018	CIN	MLB	24	1.50	6.75	3.59	0.1	93.9	55	15.3	49.3
2019	CIN	MLB	25	1.41	4.67	4.71	0.1	93.7	50.1	10.1	44.9

Lucas Sims, continued

Pitch Shape vs LHH

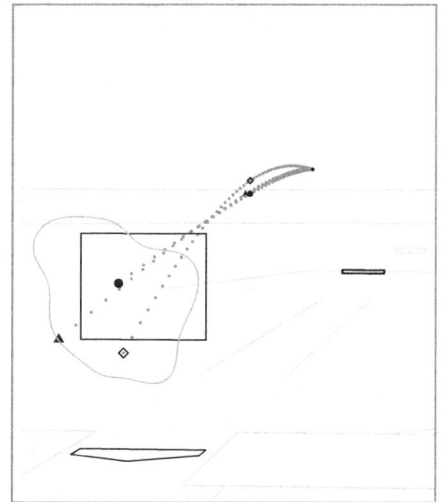

Pitch Shape vs RHH

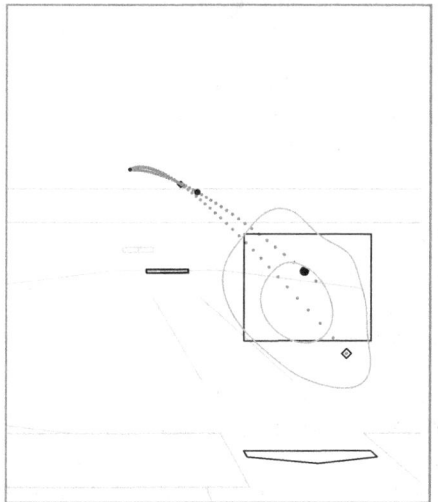

Type	Frequency	Velocity	H Movement	V Movement
● Fastball	42.9%	92.8 [101]	-4.5 [110]	-15.8 [100]
□ Sinker	12.5%	93 [103]	-10 [121]	-16.3 [113]
+ Cutter	5.4%	89.7 [106]	4.8 [117]	-24.3 [98]
▲ Changeup	11.9%	86.5 [104]	-12.4 [94]	-29.9 [92]
× Splitter				
▽ Slider				
◇ Curveball	27.2%	80.3 [107]	12.1 [118]	-42.8 [112]
✦ Slow Curveball				
✱ Knuckleball				
▼ Screwball				

Reds Player Analysis - 85

Matt Wisler RHP

Born: 09/12/92 Age: 26 Bats: R Throws: R
Height: 6'3" Weight: 210 Origin: Round 7, 2011 Draft (#233 overall)

YEAR	TEAM	LVL	AGE	W	L	SV	G	GS	IP	H	HR	BB/9	K/9	K	GB%	BABIP
2016	GWN	AAA	23	2	1	0	4	4	26²	27	3	1.7	7.4	22	52%	.296
2016	ATL	MLB	23	7	13	1	27	26	156²	159	26	2.8	6.6	115	42%	.279
2017	GWN	AAA	24	7	5	0	18	14	93²	101	7	1.9	6.1	64	44%	.310
2017	ATL	MLB	24	0	1	0	20	1	32¹	43	5	3.6	6.1	22	33%	.342
2018	ATL	MLB	25	1	1	0	7	3	26²	30	6	1.7	7.1	21	28%	.300
2018	GWN	AAA	25	4	4	0	13	13	70	79	6	1.8	8.4	65	48%	.348
2018	LOU	AAA	25	1	1	0	8	2	19²	19	0	1.4	9.6	21	36%	.339
2018	CIN	MLB	25	0	0	0	11	0	13¹	11	2	1.4	7.4	11	42%	.231
2019	CIN	MLB	26	2	2	0	31	0	32¹	31	5	3.0	8.8	31	41%	.294

Breakout: 30% Improve: 47% Collapse: 19% Attrition: 20% MLB: 86%
Comparables: Justin Grimm, Gavin Floyd, Taylor Buchholz

The twice-traded former prospect found himself in the Louisville bullpen after being a secondary piece in a trade for a secondary player. Air it out in short bursts, they said. Your stuff will play up, they said. Yet, try as he might, not only did Wisler's velocity not pick up out of the 'pen, it actually went down to the lowest level of his career. Faced with the specter of more long bus rides if he couldn't figure out a plan to get big league hitters out, Wisler did the only thing he could: He threw as many sliders as he possibly could. In his 11 appearances for the Reds between August and September, he threw the pitch nearly 55 percent of the time and it enough to save his 40-man spot for at least another offseason.

YEAR	TEAM	LVL	AGE	WHIP	ERA	DRA	WARP	MPH	FB%	WHF	CSP
2016	GWN	AAA	23	1.20	3.71	4.77	0.2				
2016	ATL	MLB	23	1.33	5.00	4.62	1.3	95.1	59.3	10.1	45.6
2017	GWN	AAA	24	1.29	3.56	4.04	1.7				
2017	ATL	MLB	24	1.73	8.35	7.24	-0.7	94.3	55.9	10.1	46.1
2018	ATL	MLB	25	1.31	5.40	3.99	0.3	94.4	53.4	10.2	49.5
2018	GWN	AAA	25	1.33	4.37	3.25	1.8				
2018	LOU	AAA	25	1.12	1.83	3.43	0.5				
2018	CIN	MLB	25	0.98	2.03	4.26	0.1	93.4	42.1	12.2	51.2
2019	CIN	MLB	26	1.29	4.25	4.30	0.2	94.3	57.4	10.4	48.5

Matt Wisler, continued

Pitch Shape vs LHH

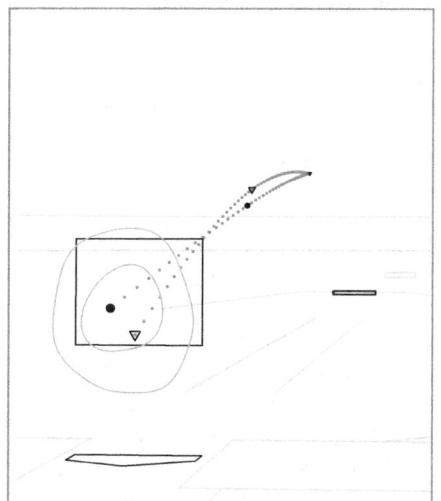

Pitch Shape vs RHH

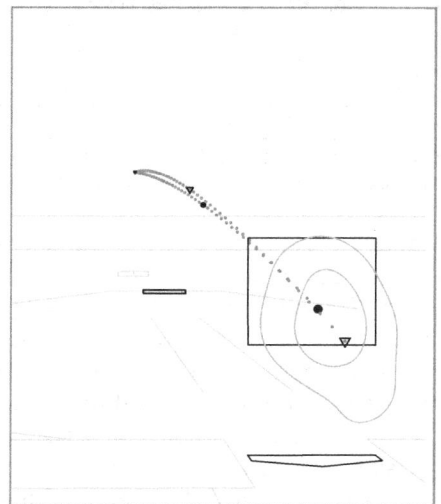

Type	Frequency	Velocity	H Movement	V Movement
● Fastball	46.1%	92.8 [101]	-6.1 [103]	-15.3 [102]
☐ Sinker	3.6%	92.6 [101]	-10.4 [118]	-14.3 [120]
+ Cutter				
▲ Changeup	0.5%	87.3 [108]	-12.2 [95]	-19.1 [124]
✕ Splitter				
▽ Slider	45.6%	82.3 [91]	7.4 [111]	-36 [91]
◇ Curveball	4.1%	77.8 [98]	7.4 [98]	-45.2 [106]
⊕ Slow Curveball				
✱ Knuckleball				
▼ Screwball				

Alex Wood LHP

Born: 01/12/91   Age: 28   Bats: R   Throws: L
Height: 6'4"   Weight: 215   Origin: Round 2, 2012 Draft (#85 overall)

YEAR	TEAM	LVL	AGE	W	L	SV	G	GS	IP	H	HR	BB/9	K/9	K	GB%	BABIP
2016	LAN	MLB	25	1	4	0	14	10	60^1	56	5	3.0	9.8	66	55%	.319
2017	LAN	MLB	26	16	3	0	27	25	152^1	123	15	2.2	8.9	151	54%	.267
2018	LAN	MLB	27	9	7	0	33	27	151^2	143	14	2.4	8.0	135	50%	.293
2019	CIN	MLB	28	8	7	0	34	19	124	112	15	3.0	9.3	128	50%	.293

Breakout: 21%   Improve: 49%   Collapse: 25%   Attrition: 5%   MLB: 96%
Comparables: Brandon Webb, Roy Halladay, Johnny Cueto

At the risk of sounding lazy, you could probably CTRL+C everything from Wood's 2017 Annual comment and CTRL+V into this space, as the last two seasons worth of stats for the lefty's career have basically been the pitching version of the Spiderman meme. However instead of declining velocity leading to late season struggles, Wood's gas remained fairly consistent this year, and he managed to combat a second-half swoon by folding in his slider over a third of the time—the highest usage of his career. An ill-fated shift to the bullpen is a decision that manager Dave Roberts would like to have back, as Wood served up three taters in less than seven innings of work, ignominiously topping the reliever leaderboard (hmm click, hold and drag to trash). The former Georgia Bulldog will now have to spend his walk year in an environment more suited to giving up homers, after becoming collateral in a salary dump to the Reds.

YEAR	TEAM	LVL	AGE	WHIP	ERA	DRA	WARP	MPH	FB%	WHF	CSP
2016	LAN	MLB	25	1.26	3.73	2.56	1.9	92.7	53	10.9	45.6
2017	LAN	MLB	26	1.06	2.72	2.89	4.5	94.0	50.4	12.5	45.1
2018	LAN	MLB	27	1.21	3.68	3.41	3.3	91.4	43.1	11.6	47.2
2019	CIN	MLB	28	1.23	3.81	3.87	1.7	92.0	47.3	11.9	46.3

Alex Wood, continued

Pitch Shape vs LHH

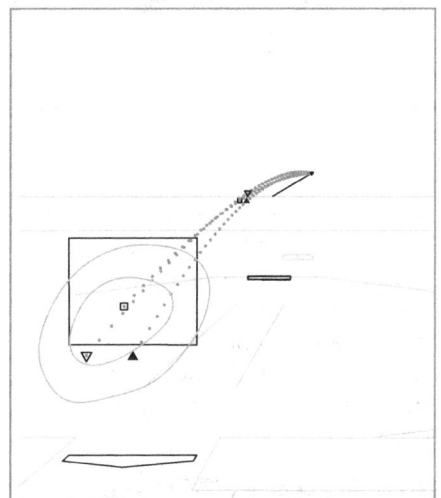

Pitch Shape vs RHH

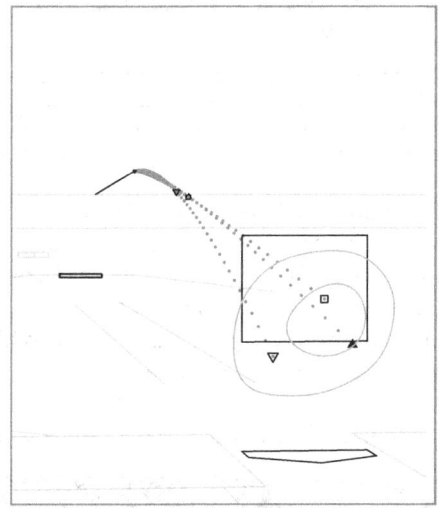

Type	Frequency	Velocity	H Movement	V Movement
● Fastball	0.1%	90.8 [95]	4.6 [110]	-14.4 [104]
□ Sinker	43.0%	90.4 [90]	10.6 [117]	-18 [108]
+ Cutter				
▲ Changeup	26.2%	84.3 [96]	13.2 [90]	-30 [92]
× Splitter				
▽ Slider	30.7%	82.8 [93]	-1.5 [86]	-37.5 [87]
◇ Curveball				
◈ Slow Curveball				
✻ Knuckleball				
▼ Screwball				

Jonathan India 3B

Born: 12/15/96 Age: 22 Bats: R Throws: R
Height: 6'1" Weight: 200 Origin: Round 1, 2018 Draft (#5 overall)

YEAR	TEAM	LVL	AGE	PA	R	2B	3B	HR	RBI	BB	K	SB	CS	AVG/OBP/SLG
2018	GRV	RK	21	62	11	2	1	3	12	15	12	1	0	.261/.452/.543
2018	DYT	A	21	112	17	7	0	3	11	13	28	5	0	.229/.339/.396
2019	CIN	MLB	22	251	22	8	0	7	25	18	83	2	1	.148/.211/.279

Breakout: 9% Improve: 11% Collapse: 0% Attrition: 10% MLB: 11%
Comparables: Jesus Guzman, Kyle Kubitza, Steven Souza

The word "kal" means both "yesterday" and "tomorrow" in Hindi, which seems appropriate when talking about India. A low-ceiling, high-floor college bat, India was chosen fifth overall in last year's draft based less on his potential to improve from yesterday to tomorrow than on his ability to continue the solid production of his Gator heyday. He's an advanced hitter with a solid approach, average power, decent speed and a capable if uninspiring glove at the hot corner. India's masala of average-or-better skills makes him a safe bet to be an everyday big leaguer, and a poor bet to become a superstar.

YEAR	TEAM	LVL	AGE	PA	DRC+	VORP	BABIP	BRR	FRAA	WARP
2018	GRV	RK	21	62	161	6.2	.290	0.6	3B(12): -0.6, SS(2): -0.2	0.4
2018	DYT	A	21	112	104	7.0	.292	1.5	3B(21): 2.4, SS(4): -0.1	0.6
2019	CIN	MLB	22	251	26	-15.8	.188	-0.1	3B 0, SS 0	-1.7

Jordan Patterson 1B

Born: 02/12/92   Age: 27   Bats: L   Throws: L
Height: 6'4"   Weight: 215   Origin: Round 4, 2013 Draft (#109 overall)

YEAR	TEAM	LVL	AGE	PA	R	2B	3B	HR	RBI	BB	K	SB	CS	AVG/OBP/SLG
2016	ABQ	AAA	24	495	75	24	7	14	61	47	118	10	0	.293/.376/.480
2016	COL	MLB	24	19	1	1	0	0	2	1	1	0	1	.444/.474/.500
2017	ABQ	AAA	25	542	78	32	7	26	92	36	128	3	5	.283/.348/.539
2018	ABQ	AAA	26	480	77	23	2	26	76	42	128	6	2	.271/.367/.525
2019	CIN	MLB	27	251	29	11	1	11	34	17	73	2	1	.218/.298/.416

Breakout: 1%   Improve: 15%   Collapse: 14%   Attrition: 19%   MLB: 31%
Comparables: Christian Walker, Daniel Dorn, Juan Miranda

When you've got a type, you've got a type. The Rockies seem to produce a never-ending stream of corner guys with just enough bat to intrigue but not quite enough consistency or defensive value to grab firm hold of a spot on the 25-man roster. Exhibit infinity: Jordan Patterson. He crushed right-handed pitching again at Triple-A last year, ho-hummed his at-bats against lefties and managed to stand competently in both right field and at first base for a majority of the year. And speaking of types, if that sounds a lot like what Jay Bruce does, minus about $13.5 million in guaranteed salary commitment, congratulations! You're a Mets executive now. Wait…no. Now you're a Reds executive! Whew, the life of a journeyman minor leaguer can be confusing.

YEAR	TEAM	LVL	AGE	PA	DRC+	VORP	BABIP	BRR	FRAA	WARP
2016	ABQ	AAA	24	495	111	19.6	.370	1.5	RF(76): 15.6, 1B(38): 0.4	2.4
2016	COL	MLB	24	19	96	0.9	.471	-0.6	RF(5): -0.3, LF(2): -0.2	-0.1
2017	ABQ	AAA	25	542	107	17.4	.330	-0.2	1B(84): 0.7, RF(39): -1.7	0.6
2018	ABQ	AAA	26	480	118	21.0	.328	0.3	1B(71): 1.1, RF(44): -2.9	1.0
2019	CIN	MLB	27	251	96	4.1	.274	-0.2	1B 0, RF 1	0.5

Nick Senzel 3B

Born: 06/29/95 Age: 24 Bats: R Throws: R
Height: 6'1" Weight: 205 Origin: Round 1, 2016 Draft (#2 overall)

YEAR	TEAM	LVL	AGE	PA	R	2B	3B	HR	RBI	BB	K	SB	CS	AVG/OBP/SLG
2016	BIL	RK	21	41	3	1	0	0	4	6	5	3	0	.152/.293/.182
2016	DYT	A	21	251	38	23	3	7	36	32	49	15	7	.329/.415/.567
2017	DAY	A+	22	272	41	26	2	4	31	23	54	9	2	.305/.371/.476
2017	PEN	AA	22	235	40	14	1	10	34	26	43	5	4	.340/.413/.560
2018	LOU	AAA	23	193	23	12	2	6	25	19	39	8	2	.310/.378/.509
2019	CIN	MLB	24	431	57	22	1	17	55	37	103	9	4	.267/.332/.460

Breakout: 12%   Improve: 38%   Collapse: 8%   Attrition: 26%   MLB: 63%
Comparables: Vince Belnome, Ryan Rua, Rob Refsnyder

Senzel's stock continued to rise as quickly as he did through the minor leagues until a series of injuries conspired to keep the 2016 first-rounder sidelined for the rest of the 2018 season. In May, it was vertigo. In June, it was a torn tendon in his right index finger. In October, it was surgery to remove bone spurs from his elbow. When healthy, he has consistently managed to do what we've come to expect from Senzel: all-around offensive success. He hit even more line drives and avoided repeating the ground-ball spike he saw in Double-A in 2017. The only question marks that remain are health-related and position-related. The Reds first sought to try him at the keystone with Eugenio Suarez entrenched at third in Cincinnati. And while that's still a possibility, they have also hinted at trying him at either center field or shortstop—and just the fact that they're trying it speaks volumes about his athleticism at the hot corner. However it shakes out, you don't have to worry about his bat nor do you have to worry about his defense. Save your worries for which God to pray to in order for Senzel to remain on the field long enough to establish himself as a star.

YEAR	TEAM	LVL	AGE	PA	DRC+	VORP	BABIP	BRR	FRAA	WARP
2016	BIL	RK	21	41	50	-1.5	.172	0.1	3B(10): 1.0	0.0
2016	DYT	A	21	251	181	34.0	.392	1.6	3B(56): 3.2	3.2
2017	DAY	A+	22	272	152	24.5	.378	1.3	3B(60): 5.1	2.4
2017	PEN	AA	22	235	169	26.5	.391	-0.5	3B(56): 1.7	2.2
2018	LOU	AAA	23	193	150	19.5	.367	1.9	2B(28): -0.8, 3B(14): 0.8	1.6
2019	CIN	MLB	24	431	108	20.0	.321	0.1	CF -1, 3B 1	2.0

Jose Siri CF

Born: 07/22/95 Age: 23 Bats: R Throws: R
Height: 6'2" Weight: 175 Origin: International Free Agent, 2012

YEAR	TEAM	LVL	AGE	PA	R	2B	3B	HR	RBI	BB	K	SB	CS	AVG/OBP/SLG
2016	DYT	A	20	87	5	3	0	0	3	2	34	3	2	.145/.163/.181
2016	BIL	RK	20	255	52	12	8	10	35	8	66	17	4	.320/.348/.560
2017	DYT	A	21	552	92	24	11	24	76	33	130	46	12	.293/.341/.530
2018	DAY	A+	22	126	15	9	2	1	9	4	32	9	1	.261/.280/.395
2018	PEN	AA	22	283	42	8	9	12	34	24	91	14	5	.229/.300/.474
2019	CIN	MLB	23	165	20	4	2	7	18	4	57	6	2	.190/.209/.373

Breakout: 11%   Improve: 21%   Collapse: 2%   Attrition: 12%   MLB: 24%
Comparables: Teoscar Hernandez, Franchy Cordero, Kirk Nieuwenhuis

We call them "tools," but in Siri's case it might be better to think of his tremendous natural gifts as "parts." His plus glove in center field? That's a part. His blazing speed, his cannon arm, the way his bat blurs as it whips through the zone? A bunch of parts. The easy power in his swing, the loft and backspin he generates as he launches a batting practice fastball into orbit? Those, too, are parts, all gleaming with a cold, sinister, yet strangely alluring light. His need to swing at every pitch in sight? That's not a part. That's the assembly line, and it's broken. Last year as a 23-year-old in Double-A, Siri struck out in nearly a third of his plate appearances. Until that gets fixed the sum of his parts will be infinitely greater than the whole. Raw talent and a bad approach can sometimes turn into Javier Baez; more frequently, it becomes Junior Lake.

YEAR	TEAM	LVL	AGE	PA	DRC+	VORP	BABIP	BRR	FRAA	WARP
2016	DYT	A	20	87	8	-8.9	.240	0.6	CF(17): 1.7, RF(9): -0.2	-0.6
2016	BIL	RK	20	255	123	25.2	.404	3.9	RF(33): 4.6, CF(21): 5.4	1.9
2017	DYT	A	21	552	135	49.1	.349	7.4	CF(103): 15.7, RF(9): 1.5	5.6
2018	DAY	A+	22	126	90	2.2	.341	1.1	CF(26): 0.4	0.1
2018	PEN	AA	22	283	91	15.0	.301	2.2	CF(59): -3.9	-0.1
2019	CIN	MLB	23	165	39	-4.4	.243	1.3	CF 1	-0.4

Taylor Trammell OF

Born: 09/13/97   Age: 21   Bats: L   Throws: L
Height: 6'2"   Weight: 195   Origin: Round 1, 2016 Draft (#35 overall)

YEAR	TEAM	LVL	AGE	PA	R	2B	3B	HR	RBI	BB	K	SB	CS	AVG/OBP/SLG
2016	BIL	RK	18	254	39	9	6	2	34	23	57	24	7	.303/.374/.421
2017	DYT	A	19	571	80	24	10	13	77	71	123	41	12	.281/.368/.450
2018	DAY	A+	20	461	71	19	4	8	41	58	105	25	10	.277/.375/.406
2019	*CIN*	*MLB*	*21*	*251*	*25*	*5*	*1*	*6*	*24*	*17*	*75*	*7*	*2*	*.180/.235/.296*

Breakout: 14%   Improve: 28%   Collapse: 1%   Attrition: 13%   MLB: 29%
Comparables: Anthony Gose, Jake Marisnick, Victor Robles

The athletic, toolsy stereotype applies to Trammell, who's already shown double-plus speed and the potential for above-average power. Although his arm is a bit weak for center field and he takes routes in the outfield that make you think he accidentally set Waze to avoid highways, his combination of jaw-dropping raw skills is enough to make any national prospect writer fawn over him in GIF form. Trammell came away from the Futures Game with some Hardware and some notoriety as well: he celebrated a home run in the bottom of the eighth inning by flashing two fingers at the dugout, to represent his second bomb of the game, only it didn't actually clear the wall. He wasn't nearly as dynamic during his season in the FSL. We know there's clear star potential here, but whether he reaches that ceiling depends on how much consistency he can show on a game-to-game or week-to-week basis.

YEAR	TEAM	LVL	AGE	PA	DRC+	VORP	BABIP	BRR	FRAA	WARP
2016	BIL	RK	18	254	92	15.1	.396	2.7	LF(39): 0.5, CF(11): 2.1	0.2
2017	DYT	A	19	571	126	41.6	.345	3.1	LF(104): -3.7, CF(17): -0.9	2.0
2018	DAY	A+	20	461	126	26.4	.358	-0.8	CF(60): -1.7, LF(29): 4.5	1.7
2019	*CIN*	*MLB*	*21*	*251*	*38*	*-9.8*	*.231*	*0.7*	*CF 0, LF 1*	*-0.9*

Brandon Finnegan LHP

Born: 04/14/93 Age: 26 Bats: L Throws: L
Height: 5'11" Weight: 212 Origin: Round 1, 2014 Draft (#17 overall)

YEAR	TEAM	LVL	AGE	W	L	SV	G	GS	IP	H	HR	BB/9	K/9	K	GB%	BABIP
2016	CIN	MLB	23	10	11	0	31	31	172	150	29	4.4	7.6	145	41%	.256
2017	CIN	MLB	24	1	1	0	4	4	13	9	1	9.0	11.1	16	53%	.276
2018	CIN	MLB	25	0	3	0	5	5	20^2	27	5	6.5	6.1	14	40%	.319
2018	LOU	AAA	25	2	10	0	28	9	67^2	90	10	5.3	7.6	57	36%	.369
2019	CIN	MLB	26	1	2	0	31	0	32^1	29	5	5.1	8.9	32	40%	.288

Breakout: 22%   Improve: 58%   Collapse: 13%   Attrition: 20%   MLB: 85%
Comparables: Andrew Miller, Jerome Williams, Mike Wood

Finnegan suffered another shoulder injury in 2017, but the Reds still held out some hope he could contribute as a starter at the outset of last season. After 14 mostly terrible starts spread between Cincinnati and Louisville, that dream finally died and he was shifted to the Triple-A bullpen. It would have been easy to imagine a scenario where the diminutive left-hander reclaimed his velocity in short bursts and started mowing down minor league bats on his way back to major-league redemption. Yet Finnegan struggled just as badly in the bullpen and wasn't heard from again—leaving his future up in the air, like so many of the batted balls hit against him.

YEAR	TEAM	LVL	AGE	WHIP	ERA	DRA	WARP	MPH	FB%	WHF	CSP
2016	CIN	MLB	23	1.36	3.98	5.90	-1.1	94.6	66.1	10.3	45.6
2017	CIN	MLB	24	1.69	4.15	5.31	0.0	96.0	69.8	13	42.1
2018	CIN	MLB	25	2.03	7.40	7.64	-0.6	92.9	65.8	7.4	48.1
2018	LOU	AAA	25	1.92	7.05	5.40	0.0				
2019	CIN	MLB	26	1.48	5.27	5.08	-0.1	94.1	67.5	10.2	46.3

Hunter Greene   RHP

Born: 08/06/99   Age: 19   Bats: R   Throws: R
Height: 6'4"   Weight: 215   Origin: Round 1, 2017 Draft (#2 overall)

YEAR	TEAM	LVL	AGE	W	L	SV	G	GS	IP	H	HR	BB/9	K/9	K	GB%	BABIP
2018	DYT	A	18	3	7	0	18	18	68^1	66	6	3.0	11.7	89	43%	.353
2019	CIN	MLB	19	3	4	0	13	13	48^2	48	8	4.3	9.5	52	40%	.322

Breakout: 1%   Improve: 1%   Collapse: 0%   Attrition: 1%   MLB: 1%
Comparables: Kolby Allard, Vicente Campos, Roberto Osuna

Greene, the Reds' top selection in the 2017 draft, has an electric fastball that can routinely top 100 mph and a slider that projects as plus. And despite that, he wasn't as dominant as was expected in his full-season debut. Ultimately, even 102 and 103 can be turned around with authority if it's true—and Spandau Ballet couldn't have laid in it there much more earnestness. As spring turned to summer, Greene turned up the heat on opposing batters, but unfortunately he inadvertently turned up the heat on his elbow ligament at the same time. After allowing one run or fewer in his last five starts, Greene was shut down for the season with a UCL sprain. Opting for rest and rehab, Greene will look to develop his secondary pitches and avoid the knife, in no particular order, during 2019.

YEAR	TEAM	LVL	AGE	WHIP	ERA	DRA	WARP	MPH	FB%	WHF	CSP
2018	DYT	A	18	1.30	4.48	3.69	1.2				
2019	CIN	MLB	19	1.47	4.95	5.38	0.0				

Vladimir Gutierrez RHP

Born: 09/18/95 Age: 23 Bats: R Throws: R
Height: 6'0" Weight: 190 Origin: International Free Agent, 2016

YEAR	TEAM	LVL	AGE	W	L	SV	G	GS	IP	H	HR	BB/9	K/9	K	GB%	BABIP
2017	DAY	A+	21	7	8	0	19	19	103	108	10	1.7	8.2	94	42%	.320
2018	PEN	AA	22	9	10	0	27	27	147	139	18	2.3	8.9	145	46%	.298
2019	CIN	MLB	23	0	1	0	10	0	10	10	1	3.0	9.2	11	41%	.294

Breakout: 9%   Improve: 14%   Collapse: 25%   Attrition: 34%   MLB: 44%
Comparables: Felix Jorge, Chih-Wei Hu, Brett Kennedy

Gutierrez was signed out of Cuba, had no problem flashing dominance at High-A in 2017 and then held his own for a full season at Double-A in 2018. There's a lot to like if he can continue his steady climb, especially if he keeps maintaining (or improving) his walk and strikeout rates. He still struggles with consistency in his delivery, but he has the ceiling of a no. 4 starter and the durability to last in a rotation even if the results leave you wanting more. Worse comes to worst, his curve and a fastball that would hopefully play up in short bursts should guarantee him a spot in the bullpen.

YEAR	TEAM	LVL	AGE	WHIP	ERA	DRA	WARP	MPH	FB%	WHF	CSP
2017	DAY	A+	21	1.23	4.46	4.71	0.7				
2018	PEN	AA	22	1.20	4.35	3.75	2.7				
2019	CIN	MLB	23	1.24	3.98	4.08	0.1				

Tony Santillan RHP

Born: 04/15/97 Age: 22 Bats: R Throws: R
Height: 6'3" Weight: 240 Origin: Round 2, 2015 Draft (#49 overall)

YEAR	TEAM	LVL	AGE	W	L	SV	G	GS	IP	H	HR	BB/9	K/9	K	GB%	BABIP
2016	BIL	RK	19	1	0	0	8	8	39	32	4	3.7	10.6	46	46%	.292
2016	DYT	A	19	2	3	0	7	7	30^1	27	3	7.1	11.3	38	38%	.338
2017	DYT	A	20	9	8	0	25	24	128	104	9	3.9	9.0	128	45%	.281
2018	DAY	A+	21	6	4	0	15	15	86^2	81	5	2.3	7.6	73	44%	.298
2018	PEN	AA	21	4	3	0	11	11	62^1	65	8	2.3	8.8	61	46%	.315
2019	CIN	MLB	22	0	1	0	10	0	10	10	2	4.9	9.0	11	40%	.294

Breakout: 12% Improve: 17% Collapse: 8% Attrition: 17% MLB: 33%
Comparables: Jake Thompson, Jayson Aquino, Greg Reynolds

Santillan has the name of a tertiary character in a Sopranos episode. And while the flamethrowing right-hander isn't from New Jersey or even New York, we can give him a mafioso nickname all the same. The Nutcracker hails from Seguin, TX, home to the world's largest nutcracker museum. He's been adding velocity and command to his heavy, sinking fastball, cracking more than a few bats along the way. He complements the heater with a hard slider, catching batters swinging over top as they anticipate the fastball. One thing he hasn't cracked thus far? The changeup. It flashes average but is inconsistent and often too firm. He might not miss enough bats to be more than an innings-eating middle of the rotation arm when it's all said and done, but that's not bad work for a character actor.

YEAR	TEAM	LVL	AGE	WHIP	ERA	DRA	WARP	MPH	FB%	WHF	CSP
2016	BIL	RK	19	1.23	3.92	2.36	1.5				
2016	DYT	A	19	1.68	6.82	3.51	0.6				
2017	DYT	A	20	1.25	3.38	4.17	1.6				
2018	DAY	A+	21	1.19	2.70	5.03	0.3				
2018	PEN	AA	21	1.30	3.61	4.19	0.8				
2019	CIN	MLB	22	1.49	5.43	5.20	0.0				

LINEOUTS

Hitters

HITTER	POS	TEAM	LVL	AGE	PA	R	2B	3B	HR	RBI	BB	K	SB	CS	AVG/OBP/SLG	DRC+	WARP
Aristides Aquino	RF	CIN	MLB	24	1	0	0	0	0	0	0	1	0	0	.000/.000/.000	87	-0.1
	RF	PEN	AA	24	445	49	20	2	20	55	35	112	4	5	.240/.306/.448	103	0.8
Mariel Bautista	CF	BIL	Rk	20	233	43	12	4	8	37	16	29	16	3	.330/.386/.541	139	0.6
Fidel Castro	RF	DRD	Rk	19	151	21	10	6	3	22	25	42	2	2	.262/.404/.516	143	0.7
	RF	CIN	Rk	19	63	9	4	2	1	5	8	23	2	1	.315/.413/.519	118	-0.4
Christian Colon	INF	GWN	AAA	29	55	3	0	0	0	3	4	8	1	0	.204/.278/.204	62	-0.1
	INF	LVG	AAA	29	313	44	22	1	6	38	36	30	11	5	.304/.396/.459	123	1.8
Stuart Fairchild	LF	DYT	A	22	276	40	12	5	7	37	31	65	17	4	.277/.377/.460	136	1.4
	LF	DAY	A+	22	242	25	14	1	2	20	17	63	6	2	.250/.306/.350	98	-0.6
Kyle Farmer	C	OKL	AAA	27	312	37	24	1	7	36	17	50	1	1	.288/.333/.451	105	0.3
	C	LAN	MLB	27	77	1	4	1	0	9	5	15	0	0	.235/.312/.324	80	0.2
T.J. Friedl	OF	DAY	A+	22	274	40	10	4	3	35	38	44	11	4	.294/.405/.412	136	1.8
	OF	PEN	AA	22	296	47	10	3	2	16	28	56	19	5	.276/.359/.360	111	1.2
Jose Israel Garcia	SS	DYT	A	20	517	61	22	4	6	53	19	112	13	9	.245/.290/.344	84	0.3
Ibandel Isabel	1B	DAY	A+	23	420	62	11	0	35	75	36	152	1	1	.258/.333/.566	134	0.9
Sherman Johnson	2B	MOB	AA	27	79	8	5	1	0	6	11	17	1	2	.194/.316/.299	74	-0.4
	2B	SLC	AAA	27	171	32	7	4	4	14	20	47	2	0	.277/.359/.459	98	0.5
	2B	ANA	MLB	27	11	0	0	0	0	0	0	4	0	0	.000/.091/.000	65	0.0
Brian O'Grady	OF	PEN	AA	26	214	27	12	4	6	30	27	41	4	1	.258/.354/.472	124	0.1
	OF	LOU	AAA	26	162	27	9	2	8	29	12	39	5	4	.306/.365/.563	136	0.8
Alfredo Rodriguez	SS	PEN	AA	24	29	4	0	0	0	0	2	7	0	0	.192/.276/.192	61	0.0
	SS	DAY	A+	24	122	12	5	1	2	12	8	22	4	0	.207/.270/.324	69	-0.2
Mike Siani	CF	GRV	Rk	18	205	24	6	3	2	13	16	35	6	4	.288/.351/.386	118	1.0
Tyler Stephenson	C	DAY	A+	21	450	60	20	1	11	59	45	98	1	0	.250/.338/.392	117	1.5
Blake Trahan	SS	LOU	AAA	24	510	55	17	1	2	31	49	104	6	3	.245/.327/.302	83	1.3
	SS	CIN	MLB	24	14	2	0	0	0	0	0	4	0	0	.214/.214/.214	78	0.0

If **Aristides Aquino** doesn't start adding more contact or on-base skills to his one redeeming tool, he's not going to make it much further than his own initials. ⓪ In his fourth rookie ball season between the Dominican and the States, **Mariel Bautista** had his most impressive campaign to date. He's not dripping with impact tools, but he doesn't strike out much and can at least fake it in center. ⓪ It's fitting that **Fidel Castro** gets to wear red, but he also hits plenty of missiles—a nearly 35 percent line-drive rate across two levels—causing a crisis for fielders. ⓪ Tetraphobia—fear of the number four—is a fairly common superstition in many East Asian countries, and might soon be moving into MLB front offices; **Christian Colon** is just the latest example of a fourth-overall draft pick who hasn't nearly lived up to the high expectations. Fortunately, or unfortunately, he's a fifth infielder at best now. ⍟ **Stuart Fairchild** made quick work of Low-A in his first full minor-league season, but upon his promotion to the Florida State League, opposing pitchers made quick work of him due to an overly aggressive approach. ⍟ Depth is great for an organization, but perhaps not for guys like **Kyle Farmer**, who raked again in Triple-A, but can't seem to get a serious look at the big-league level. A career .295 hitter in the minors, the 28-year-old can credibly spend time at both catcher and third base. ⍟ With plus speed, range enough for center and a smooth line-drive stroke, **T.J. Friedl** is a grindy Lenny Dykstra fan who fell out of the Nevada sky when teams discovered he had red-shirted as a sophomore and was eligible to be signed after the 2016 draft. ⍟ They say development isn't linear, but **Jose Israel Garcia** increased his OPS every month he was at Dayton in his stateside debut. His developing approach and ability to stick at shortstop makes him a good bet to take a step forward in 2019. ⍟ The good news: **Ibandel Isabel** does a good impression of "Hulk smash!" by hitting lots of home runs. The bad news: his hit tool is so poor that it'll be the pitchers in the upper minors yelling that at him if he doesn't make significant strides with his contact rate. ⍟ **Sherman Johnson** has hardly blazed a trail in his career, and his contact rate in a repeat at Triple-A is worrying, given that selectivity was once his (only) calling card. ⍟ Twenty-five years ago, **Brian O'Grady** could have forged a career as a pinch-hitter and spare left fielder, but ever-growing bullpens leave him on the outside looking in at even getting the opportunity to be called a Quad-A hitter. ⍟ **Alfredo Rodriguez** is a defense-first shortstop who cost the Reds nearly $9 million to sign out of Cuba in 2016. If they'd taken that money and put it in an S&P 500 ETF, they'd have $11.4 million and lot fewer excuses to make for their poor investment. ⍟ There's a reason the Reds went well overslot on **Mike Siani** in the 2018 draft, and even if he never develops much power, the rest of his tools have enough upside to race him up their prospect list in short order. ⍟ Finally healthy after losing time to wrist, thumb and concussion problems, **Tyler Stephenson** flashed the plus arm and solid receiving skills of a big league backup and enough power projection to hope for more. ⍟ The first MLB All-Star from the University of Louisiana at Lafayette was Al Dark, who starred for the New York Giants in the early 1950's. If you add an extra L to his name, that basically sums up fellow Ragin' Cajun **Blake Trahan**'s offensive prowess.

Pitchers

PITCHER	TEAM	LVL	AGE	W	L	SV	G	GS	IP	H	HR	BB/9	K/9	K	GB%	WHIP	ERA	DRA	WARP
Anthony Bass	CHN	MLB	30	0	0	0	16	0	15^1	18	1	1.8	8.2	14	53%	1.37	2.93	4.77	0.0
	IOW	AAA	30	0	3	3	27	0	32	34	3	1.7	7.0	25	53%	1.25	3.38	3.63	0.5
Matt Bowman	SLN	MLB	27	0	2	0	22	0	23	29	4	4.3	10.2	26	51%	1.74	6.26	5.54	-0.2
	MEM	AAA	27	0	1	1	18	0	23	23	2	3.1	11.7	30	55%	1.35	4.30	1.85	0.9
Ryan Hendrix	DAY	A+	23	4	4	12	44	0	51	38	2	4.6	13.9	79	55%	1.25	1.76	2.68	1.3
Jimmy Herget	LOU	AAA	24	1	3	0	50	0	59^2	59	5	3.2	9.8	65	36%	1.34	3.47	3.69	1.0
Jesus Reyes	LOU	AAA	25	1	2	0	9	0	13^2	15	3	5.9	5.9	9	52%	1.76	5.27	5.63	-0.1
	PEN	AA	25	1	8	2	29	6	64	59	4	3.8	7.5	53	61%	1.34	3.94	4.15	0.7
	CIN	MLB	25	0	0	0	5	0	5^2	4	1	3.2	3.2	2	63%	1.06	3.18	6.68	-0.1
Lyon Richardson	GRV	Rk	18	0	5	0	11	11	29	37	3	5.0	7.4	24	41%	1.83	7.14	5.20	0.3
Jackson Stephens	LOU	AAA	24	1	1	0	16	7	44	46	4	3.3	7.2	35	42%	1.41	5.32	5.62	-0.1
	CIN	MLB	24	2	3	0	29	0	38^1	50	7	3.5	7.7	33	41%	1.70	4.93	5.43	-0.2
Robert Stephenson	LOU	AAA	25	11	6	0	20	20	113	74	12	4.5	10.8	135	38%	1.16	2.87	3.65	2.4
	CIN	MLB	25	0	2	0	4	3	11^2	17	2	9.3	8.5	11	32%	2.49	9.26	6.50	-0.2
Seth Varner	DAY	A+	26	1	0	0	1	1	6	3	1	0.0	4.5	3	44%	0.50	1.50	4.84	0.0
	PEN	AA	26	9	3	0	25	17	119^1	104	19	2.3	7.5	99	40%	1.13	3.39	3.93	1.9

Called up in June after signing a minor-league deal in the offseason, **Anthony Bass** soon put together ten straight appearances in which he did not give up a walk or a run. Then he developed a back issue, got lit up and was placed on the DL, before being unceremoniously designated for assignment upon activation. Turning 30 is tough. ⓧ After two seasons lost to elbow woes and a 50-game drug suspension, 26-year-old **Joel Bender** dominated in the Double-A 'pen but was as age-inappropriate there as Judd Nelson in The Breakfast Club. He might have found something last year that gives him LOOGY potential, unless it was just Claire's earring bringing him some long-needed good luck. ⓧ More movement off his sinker made **Matt Bowman's** slider a bat-misser, but he traded deception and control to achieve it. ⓧ Getting plenty of grounders and strikeouts are a good thing, but **Ryan Hendrix** is going to have to show that his improved control during the second half of 2018 is sustainable in the upper minors in order for him to be a realistic bullpen option for the Reds in the future. ⓧ **Jimmy Herget** was once again effective out of the Louisville pen and missed more bats than he did in his first tour of Triple-A. The Reds protected him from the Rule 5 draft last November, so expect him to start getting a taste of the majors in 2019. ⓧ You know what the Midwest is? Young and restless. **Jesus Reyes** was yet another in a long line of relievers on the Reds you probably think we made up, but whether he gets an extended chance to stick in the bullpen will depend on how many batters Jesus Walks. ⓧ **Lyon Richardson** has near-elite fastball velocity and a decent breaking pitch, making expectations high for the 2018 second-round pick,

Cincinnati Reds 2019

which makes it a good thing he doesn't concern himself with the opinions of the sheep. Ⓡ **Kevin Shackelford** started his career as a pitch-to-contact righty before seeing his strikeout rates spike in 2017. His deal with the devil finally ran out, as elbow surgery and a June release by the Reds puts his career in jeopardy. Ⓡ If there were an award for the most generic reliever in baseball, **Jackson Stephens** has a good claim for it. Former starter? Check. Fastball-slider combo? Check. Always on the verge of being sent back to Triple-A? Check. Ⓡ **Robert Stephenson** would be at home in an Imperial Stormtrooper's suit. His version of target practice may miss enough bats in the minors, but he won't fool MLB hitters with such a wild approach. Ⓡ **Seth Varner** doesn't get a lot of accolades because he's gentler on the radar gun than most, but if he doesn't cut it as a back-end starter, his .494 OPS allowed against southpaws gives him a great chance of carving out a role as a lefty killer.

Reds Prospects

The State of the System:
It's more of a fun system than a great system. But it's also a good system, even if you have no confidence that they will ever develop a pitcher.

The Top Ten:

1. Nick Senzel   IF   OFP: 70   Likely: 60
ETA: Let's try 2019 this time
Born: 06/29/95   Age: 24   Bats: R   Throws: R   Height: 6'1"   Weight: 205
Origin: Round 1, 2016 Draft (#2 overall)

The Report: Coming into the year, Senzel was considered one of the safest prospect bets in baseball. Perhaps he lacked the superstar upside of some of the big names ranked around him on the 101, but he was a moneyline favorite to be an above-average regular at the hot corner. Well, I like to say that a year is an eternity in the life of a prospect, and boy did Senzel have a year. After a Eugenio Suarez breakout in 2017, the Reds decided to experiment with Senzel at second base (and even a little at short). Next, a torn finger tendon and then elbow surgery cost him most of the season. Now, the Reds are trying him in the outfield.

But when he was on the field in 2018, he was pretty much Nick Senzel—a polished plus prospect who might make a few All-Star games. Outfield might be a bit of an adventure, but he's likely fine at second, and I imagine he can still handle third. Wherever Senzel stands, the bat should play. He is a potential .300 hitter with solid-average raw power that should play to 20+ home runs given his approach, bat control, and home park. He's still a top ten prospect in baseball, just a year older now. Run it back again.

The Risks: Medium. His injury record is a bit troubling now, but there's nothing too traumatic or tools-sapping here. He's been basically major league-ready since last spring, although I'd be a little concerned about how he might take to being moved around the field this much.

Bret Sayre's Fantasy Take: You don't get too many instances where the circumstances around a top prospect make them an actual buy-low candidate, but we may have stumbled into one here. Take advantage of the slight prospect fatigue and questions about where Senzel will ultimately play, and make sure he's valued as the certain top-10 dynasty prospect he is. A potential .290 hitter with 25 homers and 15-20 steals is plenty valuable at any position.

Cincinnati Reds 2019

2 **Taylor Trammell   OF**   OFP: 70   Likely: 60   ETA: Mid-to-late 2020
Born: 09/13/97   Age: 21   Bats: L   Throws: L   Height: 6'2"   Weight: 195
Origin: Round 1, 2016 Draft (#35 overall)

The Report: You could argue there were two different versions of Trammell on display in 2018. There was the steady but unspectacular performer in Daytona, whose tools only flashed. And then there was the Futures Game version. So let's tease them out.

The Florida State League version: Trammell remained who we thought he was, which is an athletic, still raw player who still struggles at times on the defensive side. His 2018 didn't answer as many questions in the profile as we'd like. He still has work to do to develop his hit tool and get his power into games. Trammell still takes some curious routes to balls in the outfield and has not shown enough arm to get to average for center.

The Futures Game version: HARDWARE. Incredibly athletic frame, dumping balls second tank in BP. Looks the part. This is the exact kind of profile I want to bet on despite his only okay top line numbers in the minors. Plus tools profile, can likely stick in center. Why exactly hasn't he hit in the minors again?

So how do we remedy this? Showcases are dangerous, but it isn't like what Trammell showed hasn't flashed at other times. Having your national prospect coming out party in front of literally every prospect writer may put a bit of a finger on the scale, but now everyone knows what is in there.

The Risks: Medium. The foundation of tools is solid enough to almost guarantee a major-league future. We just need to see how much power, arm, and defense are going to develop.

Bret Sayre's Fantasy Take: I'm very bullish on Trammell's dynasty value. His plate discipline remained intact as he moved up a level, and there's little reason to think it will disintegrate upon reaching the upper minors. The approach will help him tap into 20-homer power and hit for a reasonable average (think .260-.270, with upside to boot). The big selling point is the speed, though. While he probably won't be efficient enough to really run up the score in the category, 30-35 steals is achievable. In this environment, that would make him a borderline OF1/OF2, and it's a big reason why he's an easy top-20 dynasty prospect.

3 **Jonathan India   3B**   OFP: 60   Likely: 55   ETA: 2020
Born: 12/15/96   Age: 22   Bats: R   Throws: R   Height: 6'1"   Weight: 200
Origin: Round 1, 2018 Draft (#5 overall)

The Report: India is the roasted salmon of the world of top prospects; it's likely quite good, but it's not going to be what I order in your *Michelin*-starred restaurant. At the plate, India is an intelligent and adaptable hitter who won't be fooled by the same pitch twice in a row. Enough raw power gets into games to punish misplaced offerings, and he should hit a lot of doubles while chipping in 15-20 homers. His defense is nothing to write home about, but third will remain his long-term home. I spoke to a few National League scouts who weren't overly impressed with him, and I understand why. India is not as exciting as it feels like the No. 5 overall pick should be. That said, he had the best present package of skills I saw in the Midwest League in 2018.

The Risks: Low. He's more likely to end up at the low end of the spectrum but there's very little delta between India's floor and ceiling. I'll be interested to see how he handles premium velocity. Assuming he can catch up to it and that he doesn't stall out with injuries, he's a major leaguer.

Probably.

Prospects, man.

Bret Sayre's Fantasy Take: There's a fair amount of hype in dynasty circles on India, who was drafted highly by a team with a strong home park after a dynamic college season. That said, the fantasy upside with India isn't all that high. He doesn't have impact power or speed, and he'll be challenged to hit for a high average despite doing so in college this year. There's definitely a place for an infielder with all-around skills in leagues of all size—just ask those who relied on Jurickson Profar in 2018—but his limited overall upside makes him a good, but not great, dynasty prospect.

4

Hunter Greene   RHP   OFP: 60   Likely: 50   ETA: 2022
Born: 08/06/99   Age: 19   Bats: R   Throws: R   Height: 6'4"   Weight: 215
Origin: Round 1, 2017 Draft (#2 overall)

The Report: Before he sprained his UCL, Greene looked the part of the typical "pitch-and-a-half" prep arm that dominates A-ball. But the results didn't match the stuff, which is especially weird given that your typical high-pick prep arm doesn't touch 100+ as often as Greene. He's got the premium athleticism you'd expect from a prospect who could have easily been drafted as a shortstop or two-way experiment, with an uptempo delivery and lightning-fast arm. The slider is still a bit slurvy, but he commands it well enough, and—again—dude throws 103. So why didn't Greene *really* dominate the Midwest League?

Well, the heater is very true, the command fringy, and he'll telegraph the slider with his arm speed. Everything's just a bit more hittable than it should be. These aren't fatal flaws by any means, but he doesn't have a well-rounded profile like MacKenzie Gore, Shane Baz, or DL Hall—the other highly-touted prep arms in his draft class. Greene's elbow situation puts his 2019 in doubt, so that could be a year of lost development time. And the risk factor here was already higher than you'd like from just looking at his draft position. You never want to dismiss the plus athlete firing triple-digit bullets, but—and lord do I abhor this phrase—he was more of a thrower than a pitcher in 2018.

The Risks: Extreme. I had some questions about how the profile was gonna develop before the UCL sprain, which just adds additional risk.

Bret Sayre's Fantasy Take: It's not that I don't like prep arms with premium velocity, it's just that there isn't much separation between guys with this pedigree from a dynasty league standpoint. The perceived value here because of his name recognition and especially high radar gun readings is a dangerous vortex to enter, made even more perilous by a right elbow that may as well have a skull-and-crossbones tattoo on it. Yes, it's an SP2 ceiling but there is just so much that can go wrong here, and it leaves Greene as a back-end Top 101 guy (come fight me, Ben).

5 Tony Santillan RHP
OFP: 60   Likely: 50   ETA: September 2019
Born: 04/15/97   Age: 22   Bats: R   Throws: R   Height: 6'3"   Weight: 240
Origin: Round 2, 2015 Draft (#49 overall)

The Report: Santillan performed across two levels in 2018 and was fine in his first taste of Double-A. His fastball sits in the mid-90s and shows above-average movement. Santillan improved his fastball command this season as well, making the pitch a true plus offering. While his slider can have some inconsistent shape, it's a hard bat-missing offering despite that. The development of a third pitch will be the key here. Santillan's change needs further refinement, but will flash average. More consistency with the secondaries will be the deciding factor between his sticking in the middle of a rotation or being just another 95-and-a-slider reliever.

The Risks: Medium. The development of his third pitch will shape his ultimate role. As is often the case with this profile, the gap in realistic outcomes at this point is pretty wide.

Bret Sayre's Fantasy Take: Santillan is almost the polar opposite of Greene, but were I faced with a decision between the two of them today in a dynasty league, I'd take the former. His 2018 season showed more upside than originally anticipated and he could settle in as a solid SP3 if he can hold the command improvement. He'll likely be someone who stands out more in WHIP than in strikeouts, but he could still run up 175-180 per year.

6 Mike Siani OF
OFP: 55   Likely: 45   ETA: 2022
Born: 07/16/99   Age: 19   Bats: L   Throws: L   Height: 6'1"   Weight: 180
Origin: Round 4, 2018 Draft (#109 overall)

The Report: The Reds went well over slot to sign Siani, a Northeast prep bat they popped in the fourth round of last summer's draft. Well, maybe not as a "bat" per se. Siani has plus-plus athletic tools that make him as sure-shot a center fielder as you'll see in a teenager. He's a 70 runner with a near elite arm. There are questions about how much he will hit, and the swing is a tad mechanical at present, although it feels like something he'll grow out of. There's some feel for contact already too, and he was perfectly fine during what you could consider a slightly aggressive first-summer assignment.

Siani is a little bit old for his prep class, if that matters to you. He may grow into some power, though it won't be a huge part of his game. But the defensive tools are so good that he won't have to hit all that much to be a productive major leaguer. It was a little surprising that he lasted as long as he did on the draft board, and while the Reds ended up paying him like a first-round pick, they also got commensurate first-round upside.

The Risks: High. Only a short-season resume so far, questions about the bat. The athletic tools give him a bit of a floor though, if not a major-league one quite yet.

Bret Sayre's Fantasy Take: One of my favorite underrated prospects in dynasty drafts this offseason, Siani isn't your typical fourth-round pick. He's raw and risky, but he's also a potential five-category contributor in the outfield who showed a better approach at the plate than expected in his pro debut. He doesn't need to go inside the top-30 this offseason, but he probably deserves to.

7. Vladimir Gutierrez   RHP

OFP: 50   Likely: 45   ETA: Late 2019
Born: 09/18/95   Age: 23   Bats: R   Throws: R   Height: 6'0"   Weight: 190
Origin: International Free Agent, 2016

The Report: There were a couple of positive markers in Gutierrez's 2018 Southern League campaign. For starters, he was mostly fine there, striking out about a batter per inning. Now, we don't scout the statline, but performance matters a bit for this kind of profile in Double-A. His change looks better these days, with more consistent dive now, although it's still used sparingly.

The rest of the profile remains mostly unchanged from when he signed. He sits in the low-90s. The fastball is a bit of a riser, and there's generally enough armside movement to keep it off barrels. Gutierrez manipulates his curveball well. He'll show a slower roller for strikes, and then ramp up the velocity and tightness to entice chases. He doesn't always get consistent 12-5 action on it, but it's a potential above-average offering.

Gutierrez still struggles at times with his fastball command, and the heater can straighten out. He doesn't really have an offering to get grounders, and the stuff isn't good enough to live in the zone. But he has shown enough durability—along with three potentially average-or-better offerings and a bit of pitchability and polish—to project him as a back-end innings-eater type. We'll just gloss over Cincinnati's lack of success in converting this type of prospect into an actual back-end innings eater.

The Risks: Medium. He was fine though not dominant in Double-A. Has been relatively durable. Could use additional command and changeup refinement.

Bret Sayre's Fantasy Take: We started out so well with this system and now we're down to "guy who is durable and might not be a reliever." Gutierrez isn't relevant at this point outside of very deep mixed and NL leagues.

8 **Jose Siri OF** OFP: 55   Likely: 40   ETA: 2020
Born: 07/22/95   Age: 23   Bats: R   Throws: R   Height: 6'2"   Weight: 175
Origin: International Free Agent, 2012

The Report: Man, I don't know. I think there's a general feeling among the outside onlookers that "Baseball Prospectus" as a prospect-ranking entity overrates this type of player. This has now endured through four different eras of lead prospect writers. We value upside over dudes who can or have actually hit. Is that fair? Man, I don't know. I'm probably gonna have Leody Taveras 50 spots higher than anyone else. So maybe.

Leody Taveras is not Jose Siri, and this is the Reds list not the Rangers. But Siri has big tools: Plus raw, plus run, plus arm, may stick in center field, [insert overly sexual descriptors and/or your favorite #hashtag here].

We often wax philosophically about how the hardest thing to evaluate is whether a prospect will hit major-league pitching. Siri is not one of the prospects that inspires a treatise. The swing gets long in order to tap into that power. He struggles with pitch recognition. Neither of those things stop him from being hyper-aggressive. He struck out 32% of the time in Double-A. This is a known issue. There's a ticket open already. But if it clicks…

Last year Steve Givarz argued that he'd write Siri as a 70/30 if he could. Yeah, that's generally frowned upon in every era of Baseball Prospectus prospect writing, but I get it. I'll go about as wide as I can here, and really this ranking feels like throwing a dart. Honestly it's not a profile I love, except for when I do.

The Risks: Extreme. The swing and miss might eat into everything here. He's older than you think.

Bret Sayre's Fantasy Take: Imagine you're in a bar and you strike up a conversation with a woman. She casually mentions that she plays bass in a local band and you two really hit it off. You go to see her band, expecting to get a Kim Deal vibe that's always gotten you a little more excited than it should. Instead, it's a reggae cover band. You knew the risks. You should have seen it coming when she said the band's name was The Kingston Cops. Now things are just weird and the potential has soured. You can't unhear her doing backup vocals on "Get Up, Stand Up."

Anyway, don't let Siri's power/speed combination get you too excited.

9 **Jose Garcia SS** OFP: 50   Likely: 40   ETA: 2021
Born: 04/05/98   Age: 21   Bats: R   Throws: R   Height: 6'2"   Weight: 175
Origin: International Free Agent, 2017

The Report: Garcia's first season stateside started poorly. He appeared overmatched at the plate, and he didn't have much of an approach nor any discernible feel for the strike zone. As the year progressed, he quieted his hands and put together better at-bats. Tall and high waisted, his athleticism stands out on the field. It's a projectable frame and he should add good weight as he matures. Blessed with a strong arm, he has the defensive chops to stick at the six. Combine that with some sneaky pop, plus speed, and improving plate discipline, and you have a player poised for a breakout in 2019.

The Risks: High, still adjusting to pro ball, questions about the long term value of the bat.

10 Tyler Stephenson   C
OFP: 50   Likely: 40   ETA: 2021
Born: 08/16/96   Age: 22   Bats: R   Throws: R   Height: 6'4"   Weight: 225
Origin: Round 1, 2015 Draft (#11 overall)

The Report: A series of one-sentence summaries detailing how we've handled, are handling, and project to handle Tyler Stephenson's career trajectory on these lists:

2016: "All prep catchers are inherently a work in progress, but he can hit for power and he's pretty good behind the dish already."

2017: "Well that was a lost year."

2018: "What do you mean '53 games behind the plate are a new career-high?'"

2019: "All prep catchers are inherently a work in progress, and that's reflected in Stephenson's receiving, footwork, and hit tool."

2020: "There was more to dream on back when he wasn't playing, but Stephenson's strong arm, plus raw power, and developing receiving skills portend a future as a backup catcher."

The Risks: High. The track record of health is now marginally less abysmal, but there is still a lot of remaining development required here on both sides of the ball.

The Next Five:

11 T.J. Friedl   OF
Born: 08/14/95   Age: 23   Bats: L   Throws: L   Height: 5'10"   Weight: 170
Origin: Undrafted Free Agent, 2016

Friedl was at the center of one of the most glaring draft oversights in recent memory. A second-round talent, the Nevada product went unpicked in 2016 because nobody knew he was eligible. Cincinnati, who was scouting him aggressively that summer anyway, pounced on the mistake. Most draftees had already signed by that point, and the Reds—who had more money remaining in their bonus pool than any other club—gave Friedl $700,000 to sign.

On the field, Friedl is a plus runner who projects as a quality fourth outfielder. He has the speed to play center and just enough arm to handle right if needed. He battles every at bat, can take a walk, and has sufficient gap power to keep pitchers honest. He's a smart baserunner and he could post double-digit steal totals in a part-time role. There's not quite enough pop here to project him as a regular, but even in a tough time for reserve outfielders, he should get a few big-league cracks.

12 Stuart Fairchild   OF
Born: 03/17/96   Age: 23   Bats: R   Throws: R   Height: 6'0"   Weight: 190
Origin: Round 2, 2017 Draft (#38 overall)

A first-rounder back in 2017, Fairchild was a slightly undersized outfielder who destroyed the ACC as Wake Forest's center fielder. Despite lofty power numbers in college, many scouts questioned whether Fairchild's pop was the product of a small ballpark and an all-or-nothing approach that could potentially be exploited by professional arms. A year-and-a-half later, those concerns have grown. He only homered nine times in 130 minor-league games last season, and while the Florida State League isn't a great place to hit, he was far too easy of an out at that level. He's an aggressive hitter who swings and misses often, even against fringy stuff, and he will likely always struggle with quality spin.

There are things to like: Fairchild is athletic, he has a very quick bat, he's an above-average runner, and his arm is strong enough for right if he needs to shift down the defensive spectrum. But there are now legitimate reasons to think he won't hit enough to tap into his power; you might also fairly question whether the power is coming at all. If he doesn't dispel one of those notions, he'll slide off this list come 2019.

13 Jimmy Herget   RHP
Born: 09/09/93   Age: 25   Bats: R   Throws: R   Height: 6'3"   Weight: 170
Origin: Round 6, 2015 Draft (#175 overall)

Herget didn't make the majors this year—as we prognosticated on last year's list—but there isn't much left for him to accomplish in the minors. He doesn't have huge stuff. The fastball might touch 95 on occasion, but sits more 90-93, with sink and run from a near sidearm slot. His delivery is funky, uptempo, and a tough look for righties. He commands a low-80s slider well, although there isn't enough depth to consistently miss bats. It's still not really a late-inning arm, but Herget is a major league-ready bullpen piece who has gotten it done at every level.

14 Lyon Richardson   RHP
Born: 01/18/00   Age: 19   Bats: B   Throws: R   Height: 6'2"   Weight: 175
Origin: Round 2, 2018 Draft (#47 overall)

The Reds other second round arm from 2018, Richardson is a typical advanced Florida prep arm. While he doesn't feature a ton of remaining projection, the fastball sits low-90s and can touch the upper-90s, so it's not like you need to dream on the frame or a velocity bump here. The secondaries are on the raw side with the curveball at least flashing at times, and given his uptempo delivery with some late effort, you might be best off letting him try to more consistently find the plus-or-better velocity in short bursts out of the pen. That decision is a ways down the road at this point though.

15 — Tanner Rainey   RHP
Born: 12/25/92   Age: 26   Bats: R   Throws: R   Height: 6'2"   Weight: 235
Origin: Round 2, 2015 Draft (#71 overall)

The good news for Rainey is that when you throw in the upper-90s with a wipeout slider you usually get opportunities to bring down that 24.43 MLB ERA. While he wasn't exactly painting the corners in the minors, Rainey's stuff was all over the place in the majors, and his delivery suffers from endemic and severe bouts of overthrowing. In the minors, this was less of an issue when he was pumping 99 somewhere in the general vicinity of the bottom of the zone and pairing it with a low-90s slider. That's still uncommon even in la grande liga, but major leaguers see it enough to recognize when it ain't close. Any real refinement here in the control/command could make Rainey a late-inning arm, but either way, upper-90s and a slider gets opps.

Others of note:

Aristides Aquino, OF, Cincinnati Reds
Can I interest you in Jose Siri with fewer tools but more actualized game power? Aquino did a bit better in a repeat engagement in Double-A—slightly more contact, general improvement around the margins. Power is the only real standout tool here though, and while hey, I'm never gonna tell you dingers aren't cool, if Siri looks like this after his age-24 season… well, he'll be down here too, I guess. Aquino did get the briefest of looks in the majors—a function of his being on the 40-man and Joey Votto having a balky knee—but he's not a lock to get back to improve on that 100% K-rate.

Top Talents 25 and Under (born 4/1/93 or later):

1. Nick Senzel
2. Taylor Trammell
3. Jonathan India
4. Jesse Winker
5. Hunter Greene
6. Tony Santillan
7. Jose Peraza
8. Mike Siani

Cincinnati Reds 2019

9. Sal Romano

Though the Reds appear intent on moving beyond the rebuilding phase, the bulk of their young talent has not yet reached Cincinnati. Injuries have delayed the arrival of Nick Senzel, the fast-moving college bat™ who turns 24 in June. Senzel might burst out of the gate as the super-advanced hitter he's been billed as, but any slow start will raise questions about whether the club complicated his rise by foisting new defensive positions upon him. It's one thing to plan around Eugenio Suarez, but it doesn't feel like Senzel should be the tail wagged by Scooter Gennett's breakout.

We'll soon see how the Reds approach the development of fellow fast-moving college bat™ Jonathan India, also a third baseman. Trammell represents a welcome diversification of the portfolio. He's not nearly ready for the show yet, but could one day bring electricity to the top of the order.

As for the present-day top of the order, Winker might be a Bizarro Joey Votto who simply isn't allowed to work out. Before losing half his season to a shoulder injury, he showed premium plate discipline, though his slugging percentage was caught in a battle with his (admittedly excellent) OBP. While Winker likely wouldn't rank ahead of the scintillating Greene if the young hurler were fully healthy, he wins points for his steady bat and an eye that anyone can appreciate.

Jose Peraza doesn't inspire such confidence. A long-declining stock, his surface stats hinted at progress in 2018. He lifted and pulled the ball a bit more to post average-ish numbers, yet there was no discernible change in his approach to fuel any optimism going forward. He still chases too much and lacks the exceptional in-zone aggression that works for some of Atlanta's free-swingers, for instance. The result is a limp noodle of a bat that will live and die on BABIP fluctuations and the carry of fly balls down the line. Incoming hitting coach Turner Ward isn't known for any particular strategy, but a new voice in the room probably can't hurt. Regardless of how you feel about him, expect Peraza to get 600 more plate appearances to prove he deserves a role on a team that's trying.

The Reds continue to flail on the mound. Romano's inclusion here may be charitable, and could soon look silly. He gets the nod over Brandon Finnegan, Cody Reed and Lucas Sims though, because his fastball and slider do look good together and, indeed, rate well in BP's tunneling metrics. Though he took his lumps, the combination improved as the season went on. Really only in possession of two good pitches, he might benefit from the shorter outings of a Rays or playoff-Brewers style pitching plan.

Part 3: Featured Articles

The Hole in The Shift is Fixing Itself

Russell Carleton

I've been on a bit of a mission against The Shift of late. I'm not out to get The Shift for the usual reasons that people oppose it. The words "the right way to play the game" won't be found on my lips. If a team wants to pursue a strategy that is within the rules and it works, then by all means, they have my blessing (not that they need it). Instead, my concern with The Shift is a worry that it doesn't work, or at least that it has a flaw that needs fixing.

The data show that while The Shift does a decent job of preventing singles on balls in play (what it's supposed to do), it also increases the number of walks that happen in front of it, and the number of additional walks outweighs the number of singles saved. It's a problem because you can't throw a guy out if he gets to walk to first base.

But the "why" was important. It seemed that The Shift was changing the way in which pitchers pitched. We saw that there were fewer fastballs thrown in front of The Shift than we might otherwise expect, and that pitchers tended to stay out of the strike zone a little more. Not by a lot. In fact, it might not even be visible to the naked eye. The percentage of pitches that are out of the zone goes from 51.0 to 53.3 from a standard defense (two right/two left) to a full shift (three on one side). That difference stands up even after we control for the types of hitters that get shifted against. And it's enough to drive up the walk rate to where it cancels out the benefits that teams thought they were getting with The Shift… and then some.

But there was some hope. I found that when individual pitchers stayed closer to the in-zone/out-of-zone mix that they used without The Shift on, they could still get the benefits of The Shift without the walk problems. So, in theory, a team could simply figure out a way to convince its pitchers to not fall prey to the walk trap and The Shift would once again be their friend.

It's reasonable to think that some teams might be more hip to this idea than others. Maybe some figured it out a year before the others. Maybe they were better at getting the message across to their pitchers. Or, maybe no one has figured it out yet.

Warning! Gory Mathematical Details Ahead!

I used data from 2015-2017, made available through MLB's data portal, Baseball Savant. They are kind enough to note when teams are using an infield shift (three fielders on one side of second base), as opposed to a "strategic shift" (someone's playing a bit out of position, but it's not quite that drastic) or a "standard" alignment.

Since we're doing this by team, I can't just look at raw walk rates, because we know that some teams have good pitchers and others have not-so-good pitchers. Some have a mix of both. I used the log-odds ratio method to take into account a batter's general walking proclivities, and a pitcher's as well, and then shoving them into a binary logistic regression. Then, I asked the computer to generate a specific coefficient for each team's pitchers, for when they went into The Shift and how that affected their walk rate.

Using those coefficients, I was able to project what would happen if a league-average pitcher faced a league-average hitter (which we expect would produce a league-average walk rate; from 2015-2017, 7.7 percent of plate appearances ended in a walk) and then just switched his hat. Here's the top five and the bottom five:

Top 5 Teams	Projected Shift Walk Rate	Bottom 5 Teams	Projected Shift Walk Rate
Rockies	6.2%	Rangers	11.2%
Pirates	6.7%	Mets	10.4%
Indians	7.2%	Dodgers	10.2%
Astros	7.3%	Cardinals	9.9%
Braves	7.7%	Tigers	9.7%

There are probably people out there right now trying to figure out what the common thread is among the top and bottom teams. I'm sure, because this is Baseball Prospectus, people are already trying to make the case that sabermetric "early adopters" have some sort of edge here. I think that the more interesting piece is that by the time you get to fifth place in The Shift, we're at league average.

As a sanity check, I examined the issue on a pitch-by-pitch level, looking at how often pitchers threw their pitches in the GameDay strike zone, and again using the same basic methodology and getting team-specific coefficients. The names on the list re-arranged themselves, but the idea was the same, and the two lists correlated with an R of .593.

There's a reason that I don't usually do this type of leaderboard post. I don't really know what the Rockies, Pirates, Indians, Astros, and Braves have in common, or what they have that the bottom five don't. I can put a shrug emoji here and say, "Well, it must be something!" but that seems like a cop-out. Instead, I'd like to present another table and suggest that the table above doesn't even really matter anymore.

Year	League Percent Outside K Zone (Full Shift)	League Percent in K Zone (No Shift)	Difference
2015	54.1%	51.1%	3.0%
2016	53.3%	50.9%	2.4%
2017	52.6%	50.9%	1.7%
2018	52.0%	50.7%	1.3%

The hole in The Shift is fixing itself, and it's coming down really fast league wide. In my earlier work on The Shift, I suggested that until teams stopped having such a huge difference between their out-of-zone rate with and without The Shift on, there would just be too many walks for The Shift to make sense. It seems that all 30 of them have been working toward just that. I once estimated that it takes about 10 years for an idea to filter its way through baseball. At this rate, it looks like teams are going to catch up a lot faster than that. And yeah, they're all saber-smart now.

It's likely that whatever magic it was that the Rockies and Pirates had has made its way to Texas and Queens. Or is at least on its way. And if teams are committing to fixing the walk problem, then it's likely that they will continue shifting and shifting a lot.

And eventually it's going to actually make sense for them to do it.

—*Russell Carleton is a former author of Baseball Prospectus and now an analyst for the New York Mets.*

The State of the Quality Start

Rob Mains

One of the seven things you (probably) didn't know about the 2018 season is that quality starts—defined as a start lasting six or more innings with three or fewer earned runs allowed—as a percentage of total starts cratered to an all-time low of 41 percent. I want to look a little more deeply into this, since it's been a while (May of 2016, to be exact) since I've examined quality starts.

The term *quality start* is credited to *Philadelphia Inquirer* sportswriter John Lowe. It's been derided ever since he coined it in December of 1985. Three runs in six innings? That's a 4.50 ERA! In what world is that a measure of quality?

Let's start with that criticism. It's true that 3 x 9 / 6 = 4.5. (You came here for this sort of high-level math, right?) But it's also true that type of start, meeting the bare minimum for earning a quality start, is unusual. Here's the proportion of quality starts in which the pitcher lasted exactly six innings and yielded exactly three earned runs. (I'm going to confine this analysis to the 30-team era, 1998-present. Almost all data retrieved in this article is via the Baseball-Reference Play Index.)

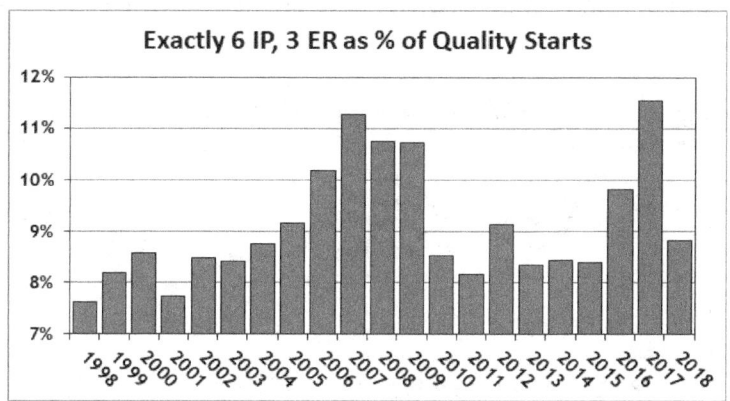

There were 1,997 quality starts in 2018. Only 176, or fewer than one in 11, featured a pitcher going six innings and allowing three earned runs. Put another way, the percentage of quality starts that resulted in a 4.50 ERA (8.8 percent) is less than half the percentage of games in which a batter hit two home runs and his team lost (22.5 percent; 237-69 won-lost). That doesn't impugn hitting two homers.

So if a 4.50 ERA isn't the norm, what is? How good are quality starts?

Pretty good, it turns out. First, on a team level:

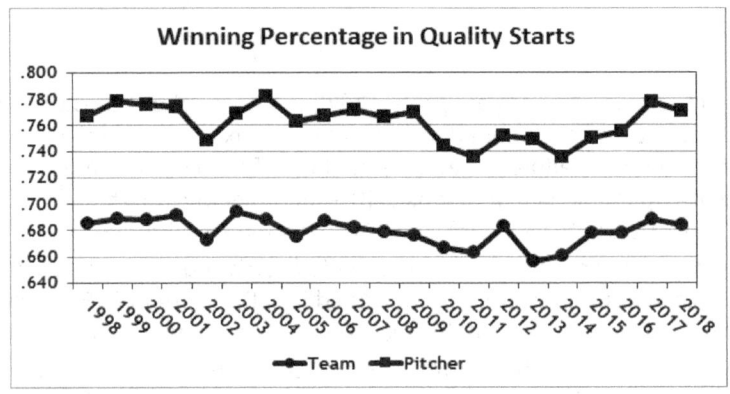

Teams receiving a quality start from their pitcher won 68.4 percent of their games in 2018, in line with the 30-team era average of 67.9 percent. A team with a .684 winning percentage wins 111 games. Getting a quality start is definitely a good thing. Individual pitchers throwing quality starts have a higher winning percentage because a big slice of team losses is assigned to a reliever.

If teams do well in quality starts, how well do the starting pitchers do? Again, very well.

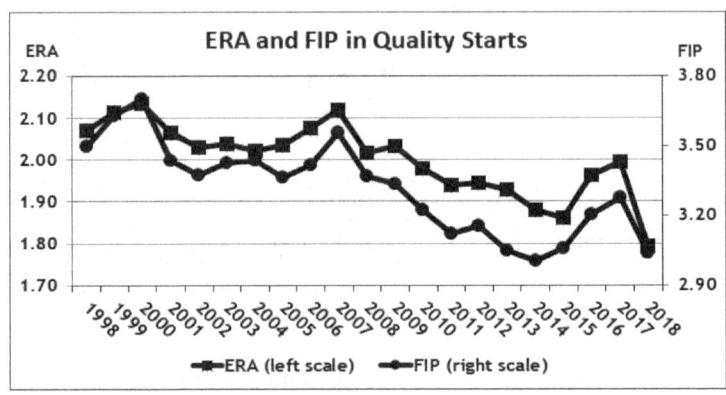

Pitchers in quality starts had a 1.79 ERA (blue line) in 2018, *the lowest in the 30-team era*. Their FIP was higher, 3.04, but still excellent. In the 30-team era, only 2014 had a lower FIP for quality starts, 3.01.

But, of course, the run environment in 2014 was different. Teams in 2014 scored 4.07 runs per game, the fewest in a non-strike year since 1976. They scored 4.45 runs per game in 2018. So surrendering a 3.04 FIP in 2018 is more impressive than 3.01 in 2014. Accordingly, let's look at ERA and FIP in quality starts relative to league averages.

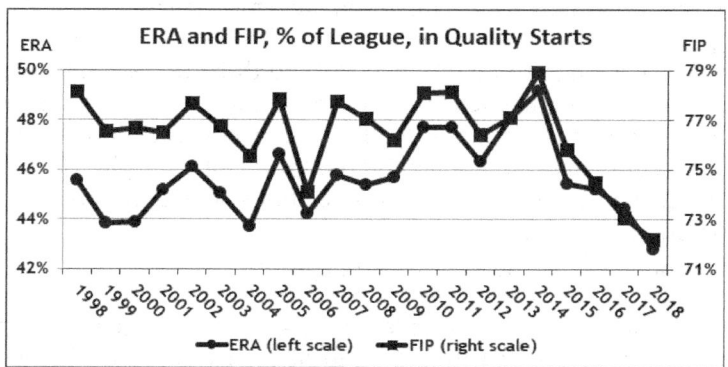

This tells a more dramatic story. Starting pitchers in 2018 gave up a 4.19 ERA and a 4.21 FIP. Starters in quality starts gave up a 1.79 ERA, 43 percent of the league average. Starters in quality starts gave up a 3.04 FIP, 72 percent of the league average. Both of these marks represent lows in the 30-team era.

The takeaway here is this: *Quality starts are better, relative to other starts, than they've ever been over the past 21 years.*

Maybe during the winter I'll look at this over a longer arc of time. For now, though, we can definitively say quality starts are the best they've ever been since the Diamondbacks and Rays joined the majors.

Yet, paradoxically, they're down.

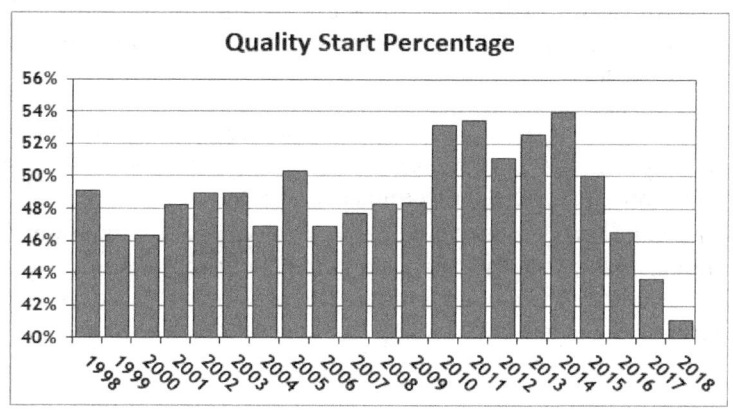

This graph covers only the 30-team era. In my article last week, though, I looked at the years 1908-2018. The result was the same. The 41 percent of starts in 2018 that were quality starts are an all-time low, well below the runners-up: 1930's 43 percent (the year teams scored an all-time record 5.55 runs per game) and last year's 44 percent.

The normal explanation for a dip in quality start percentage is an increase in scoring. When teams score a lot of runs, it's harder for starting pitchers to last six or more innings and limit opponents to three earned runs. From 1998 to 2014, the correlation between runs scored per game and the percentage of starts that were quality starts was -0.94. That means there was an extremely close relationship: More runs, fewer quality starts. Too small a sample? Go back to the start of the Expansion Era, 1961, and the relationship is even more negative, a -0.95 correlation, though 2014.

But that's broken down over the past four years:

- 2015: Runs per game increased from 4.07 to 4.25, quality start percentage decreased from 54.0 to 50.1. Yes, that's a negative relationship, but the regression model would predict a decline of 1.5 percentage points. We got 3.9 instead.
- 2016: Runs per game increased from 4.25 to 4.48, quality start percentage decreased from 50.1 to 46.6. Past experience would suggest a decline of just 1.8 percentage points. We got 3.4.
- 2017: Runs per game increased from 4.48 to 4.65, quality start percentage decreased from 46.6 to 43.6. Again, the direction's right, but the magnitude isn't. Using the relationship from 1998 to 2014, that increase in scoring should've reduced quality starts by 1.3 percentage points, not 2.9.
- 2018: Runs per game declined from 4.65 to 4.45. That should've resulted in the quality start percentage moving in the other direction, rising 1.6 points. It didn't. It fell 2.6 points, as noted, to an all-time low.

Granted, we're talking about just four years here. Maybe they're outliers. But I don't think they are. Quality starts, as noted, are as good or better than ever. But they're rarer than ever as well. And I think I know why.

To get a quality start, you need to allow three or fewer earned and pitch at least six innings. That's 18 outs. Here's a graph showing the number of starting pitchers who limited their opponents to three or fewer earned runs but got pulled after pitching at least five innings but fewer than six:

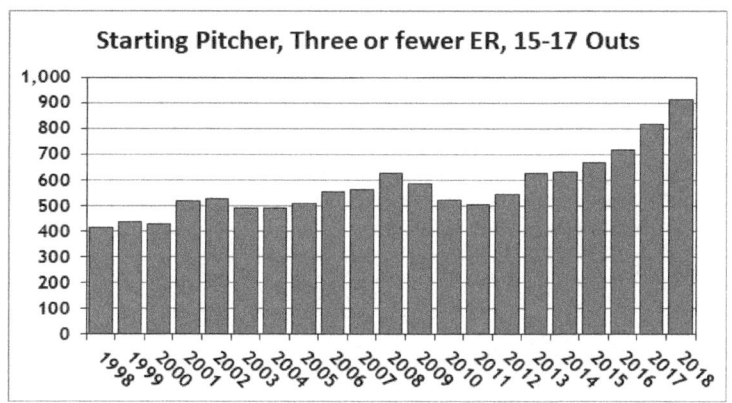

A pitcher getting 15 outs pitched five innings. A pitcher getting 16 outs pitched 5 1/3. A pitcher getting 17 outs pitched 5 2/3. More than ever before, pitchers are being removed from games in which they are within 1-3 outs of a quality start, falling just short of the six-inning finish line. Widespread acknowledgement of the times-through-the-order penalty and a flotilla of available bullpen arms is making the quality start simultaneously both more excellent and more rare.

Which is ironic, given that we saw a new post-war quality start record this season:

Rank	Pitcher	Season	Consecutive QS
1	Jacob deGrom	2018	24
2	Bob Gibson	1968	22
-	Chris Carpenter	2005	22
4	Johan Santana	2004	21
5	Luis Tiant	1968	20
-	Mike Scott	1986	20
-	Jake Arrieta	2015	20
8	Robin Roberts	1952	19
-	Tom Seaver	1973	19
-	Jack Morris	1983	19
-	Greg Maddux	1998	19
-	Josh Johnson	2010	19
-	Jon Lester	2014	19

While there have been longer streaks spread over multiple seasons, no pitcher since World War II threw more consecutive quality starts in one year than Jacob deGrom this year. The fact that he did in a year in which quality starts were the rarest they've ever been adds to the accomplishment.

—*Rob Mains is an author of Baseball Prospectus.*

Heads-Up Hacking—The First Pitch

Matthew Trueblood

Batters fell behind in a higher percentage of all plate appearances in 2018 than in any previous season for which we have pitch-by-pitch data. That kind of granular information goes back only to 1988, but we might safely assume (given all we know about baseball as it had been before that, and as it has been in the years since) that batters have *never* fallen behind at a higher rate than they did last season.

Through the 1990s, the percentage of all plate appearances that began 0-1 hovered in the high 30s and low 40s. In the 2000s, it rose steadily but slowly, through the mid-40s. In 2018, 49.8 percent of all trips to the plate began 0-1. That, as much as anything, captures in microcosm the nature of hitting in MLB today.

A countdown clock toward strike three begins ticking almost the moment a batter takes his place in the box. The league's adjusted OPS+ on the first pitch was higher in 2018 than ever before, and that has been true in most of the last 10 seasons. Batters hit .264/.289/.442 in all plate appearances in which they swung at the first pitch last season, and .241/.330/.395 in all plate appearances in which they took that first offering.

The percentage differences in batting average and isolated power there favor swinging at the first pitch by more than in any season since 1988, while the difference in on-base percentage favors taking by more than ever. If you want to get on base at a decent clip, it's a good idea to be patient, but you run the risk of missing the only chances you'll get to produce power.

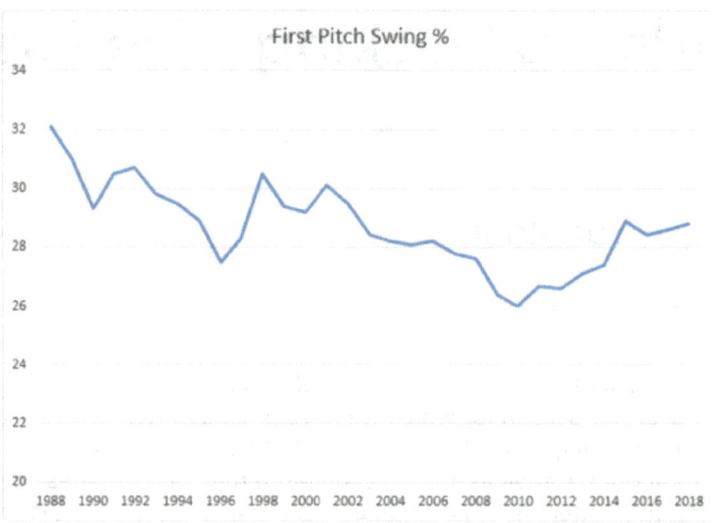

The league swung at the first pitch 28.8 percent of the time in 2018. With the isolated exception of 2015, that's the highest that number has climbed since 2002, but it might not be high enough. With the help of BP research maven Rob McQuown, I looked at the aggregate Called Strike Probability (CSProb) on the first pitch for each season since 2008, when the implementation of PITCHf/x first made measuring that possible. It's risen sharply during that period.

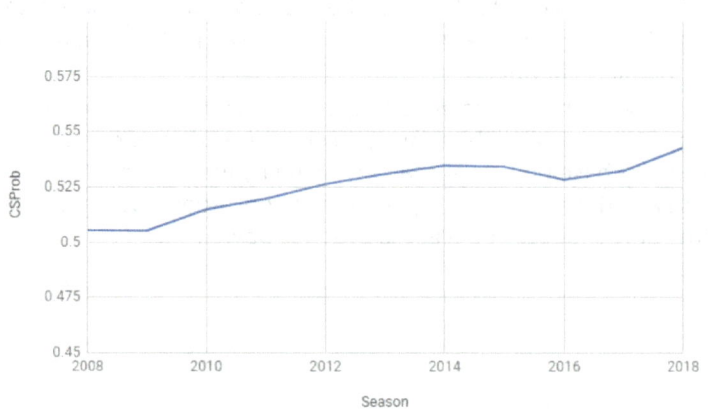

Called Strike Probability, First Pitch of PA (2008-2018)

Called Strike Probability is exactly what it sounds like: a pitch with a given CSProb has roughly that chance of being called a strike, if not swung at. In 2018, a batter who took 100 first pitches from a random sampling of the league's pitchers might expect to fall behind 54 or 55 times—up from 50 or 51 times in 2008. Almost regardless of pitch type (and, notably, especially in the case of fastballs), the first pitch tends to have more of the zone right now than ever before.

Pitchers are better at throwing strikes. They have better stuff, and believe more in their ability to miss bats within the zone. Perhaps most importantly, they know that batters are looking for one thing on the first pitch: a fastball. If they don't get it, they're likely to take the pitch. Check out how the use of sinkers and four-seamers on the first pitch has changed in a decade:

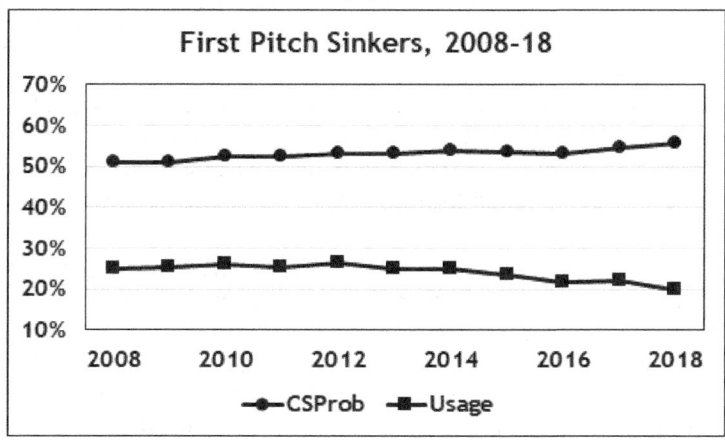

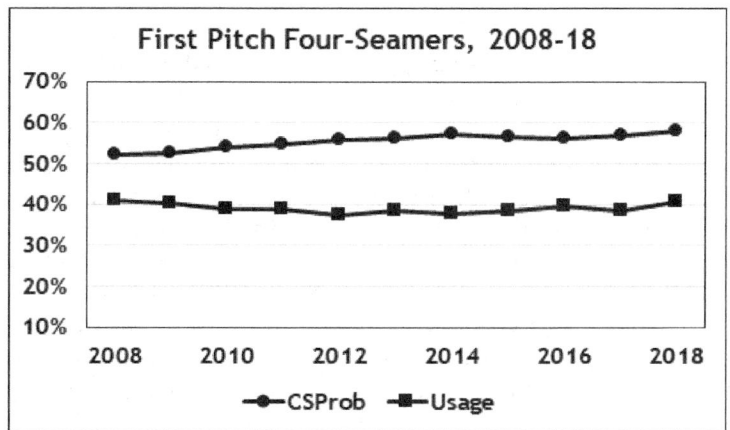

The sinker is losing its place in baseball, but the rate at which pitchers have thrown it on the first pitch hasn't dropped any faster than its usage rate in other counts. Pitchers have actually gone to their four-seamer *more* often to open counts, in the last few years, after a dip in the 2012-2015 period. What's really changed, though, and what shows up in both charts above, is that pitchers are catching more of the zone with first-pitch fastballs than they were a decade ago, or a half-decade ago. They're attacking right away, even with the pitch they know batters are expecting. The message is pretty clear: batters are being too passive.

Sliders, curves, and changeups each have more of the zone when thrown on the first pitch than they did several years ago, too, though the effect is less pronounced. Pitchers have seen the numbers; they know batters are doing better on the first pitch itself. They still feel safe throwing more and better strikes than ever before, figuring they'll come out ahead as long as they keep getting ahead to open each battle.

The Moneyball revolution brought an increased league-wide focus on OBP, which resulted in a de facto mandate to take a more patient tack at the plate. It worked very well for a while, as batters with poor plate discipline were compelled to either adjust or be expelled from the league, and pitchers with poor control were slowly weeded out.

However, concurrent with that revolution, and spurred by it in some ways, was the evolution of the pitching paradigm that now dominates the game. As batters ratcheted up their focus on inflating pitch counts and working walks, pitchers honed theirs on throwing strikes and missing bats. The league's understanding of what makes a good pitcher improved at least as much, from the mid-1990s through the mid-2000s, as its understanding of what makes a good hitter. As amphetamines and other performance-enhancing drugs were phased mostly out of the game, and as PITCHf/x broke onto the scene, individuals and teams learned how to exploit the evolved approaches of even the smartest hitters.

The ability to avoid making outs is still the most valuable one in baseball, but the magnitude of its eclipse of slugging is smaller than ever. To a greater extent than power, on-base skills derive their value from chaining—from the on-base skill levels of the players on either side of a given individual. Eleven years ago, when the housing crisis hit, people learned the hard way that the value of their homes depended a good deal on the values of their neighbors' homes. The same wasn't true, though, of their cars. So it is now, with OBP and SLG.

The global OBP in 2018 was .318. The only seasons since the Dead Ball Era in which the league got on base at a worse clip were 2013-2015, 1988, 1971-1972, and 1963-1968. This is all happening despite the aforementioned evolution of the science of hitting. It's happening despite a shift in approach and focus, one that would steer OBP ever higher, if only it were working.

Instead, it's sitting at a low ebb, and while it does so, even guys who get on base often are a little less helpful than they were 10 years ago—or 20, or 40, or 60, or 70, or 80, or 90. They're less helpful, that is, because unless there happen to be three or four other guys in the lineup who get on just as regularly, their contribution is merely to forestall the inevitable. Runs happen, increasingly, when a sudden bang happens, and that means attacking early in the count—because pitchers are sure as hell doing that.

In a league making contact on barely 75 percent of its swings, and a league in which an increasing number of pitchers can throw multiple off-speed pitches for strikes in any count, the only way to consistently generate offense is going to be aggressive. This isn't necessarily true for individuals, like Mookie Betts and Jose Ramirez, who make a lot of contact and have excellent plate discipline, and whose power comes from such natural quickness in a short stroke. Most players have to make tradeoffs, though, whether it be lowering their contact rate or raising their chase rate, in order to consistently make the quality of contact necessary to survive in today's game.

Highest %	Lowest %
Javier Baez – 48.3	Joe Mauer – 4.6
Freddie Freeman – 47.1	Mookie Betts – 9.7
Ozzie Albies – 46.3	Brett Gardner – 10.7
Jose Altuve – 44.2	Jose Ramirez – 12.0
Nick Castellanos – 44.1	Jason Kipnis – 13.8
Joey Gallo – 42.3	Jesus Aguilar – 14.5
Corey Dickerson – 40.9	Xander Bogaerts – 15.8
Salvador Perez – 40.8	Brian Dozier – 16.3
Eddie Rosario – 40.7	Mike Trout – 17.6
Nick Ahmed – 40.4	Yasmani Grandal – 17.6

Top 10 and Bottom 10 Hitters, First-Pitch Swing Rate (2018)

The question isn't which of these lists one prefers, but what they each convey, qualitatively, about the cat-and-mouse game of early-count hitting. Those top five on the left, especially, drive home the fact that for most players, getting aggressive early in the count is now key to keeping strikeout rate down and hitting for power.

For now, the message is: pitchers are coming right after batters with the nastiest stuff they've ever had. Batters had better stop giving away strike one and force hurlers to adjust, or the global OBP crisis is only going to get worse.

—*Matthew Trueblood is an author of Baseball Prospectus.*

A Hymn for the Index Stat

Patrick Dubuque

We survived without computers. I know this, because I remember the day when my dad hooked up his brand-new Atari 400 computer to the back of our 12-inch Magnavox television, and the perfect blue of the memo pad lit up for the first time. I was born just on the edge of that transitional generation, of learning cursive and balancing checkbooks and just doing math all the time, constant manual arithmetic.

It still amazes me. We learned how to sail ships without computers. We learned how to do calculus. We built towers that didn't fall down, most of the time. We engineered catapults to knock them down anyway. We built a robust system of philosophy called "utilitarianism," founded on the principle that the good of an action is evaluated by summing the effects of that action, which is the kind of formula that would make the world's mainframes crash. The whole foundation of statistics as a field is "here's math you could easily do but would die of old age first."

The fact of the matter is that there is too much math in the world to do. There are too many things changing, and too many things too small to notice, for us to handle. At some point, they become too much for the computers to handle as well, which is why we have chaos theory and undetectable earthquakes, but it's not an even fight. At some point, we fall back on intuition, and given how under-equipped we are, we're forced to bestow that intuition with some sort of supernatural superiority, the "gut feeling," that we can't prove because we can only intuit that our intuition is better.

We're all lousy at intuition, and wonderful at lying to ourselves about it. The honest truth is that computers are far better at intuition than we are, because in order to know what feels "off" you have to know what's "on." In order to do that you have to constantly reassess the average of everything, then re-rank your own experience against it.

Test your own, by comparing these three anonymous lines:

Player	G	HR	AVG	OBP	SLG
Player A	156	38	.259	.342	.535
Player B	154	38	.280	.348	.527
Player C	158	38	.266	.343	.509

These all seem like pretty similar players, right? The second one a touch more batted-ball dependent, the third a little less strong, but all pretty good hitters. And you'd be right, about the latter. Not the former.

Here's the breakdown:

- Player A: 1991 Howard Johnson, 141 DRC+
- Player B: 1996 Dean Palmer, 121 DRC+
- Player C: 2018 Giancarlo Stanton, 114 DRC+

Baseball is fortunate to have escaped the seismic shifts of so many other sports, where the talents and performances of other eras are nearly unrecognizable. (And not just other sports: try to explain the greatness of the movie Duck Soup without adjusting for era.) But they're still there, and they're nearly impossible to account for manually, without having to resort to sweeping generalizations like "steroid era" or juiced-ball era" to throw out entire swathes of production.

This is all to say that we should celebrate the index stat, that simple 100-based scale with such a humble aim: just to give context. It's hard to imagine how we lived without them for so long. Sabermetricians have always tried to make their stats look like other stats: True Average mapped to batting average, FIP molded to look like and compare to ERA. It's easy to understand the motivation—these statistics carry an emotional value in them that is hard to resist, as with the .300 hitter and the 2.00 ERA—but even they fall prey to the same loss of scale as their unadjusted counterparts. If a .300 average means different things in different years, does that hold true for a .300 True Average?

Instead, 100 doesn't say anything, except above average or below. And it does it instantly, for every season in every run environment for any statistic we want it to. We should have more index stats: K%+, so we can stop comparing Mike Clevinger's career 9.46 K/9 to Nolan Ryan's 9.55. HBP%+, so we can note that Ron Hunt was getting plunked when nobody else was getting plunked, as opposed to that imitator Brandon Guyer. Some might note how stale these references are and accuse league-adjustment as a backward-looking drive, and this is true. But we're always looking backward, always comparing the new with the expectations already set. The index stat just forces us to be honest.

There's always resistance to a new statistic, especially one so outwardly simple and so internally complex. We tend to stick with what we know, even in the case of formulas that are supposed to tell us what we know. But if your resistance is that it seems too complicated, too counterintuitive, too "black boxy," I encourage you to consider why you feel that way. Because the real world is infinitely more complicated than baseball, where all the pitches go in one basic direction and the baserunners are only allowed to travel in four directions. Baseball statistics based on mixed methodology are almost impossibly intricate. So are skyscrapers and automobiles. That's why we have computers—to take the guesswork out of them.

—*Patrick Dubuque is an author of Baseball Prospectus.*

Index of Names

Aquino, Aristides	99, 111	
Barnhart, Tucker	22	
Bass, Anthony	101	
Bautista, Mariel	99	
Blandino, Alex	24	
Bowman, Matt	101	
Casali, Curtis	26	
Castillo, Luis	52	
Castro, Fidel	99	
Colon, Christian	99	
DeSclafani, Anthony	54	
Despaigne, Odrisamer	56	
Dietrich, Derek	28	
Duke, Zach	58	
Ervin, Phil	30	
Fairchild, Stuart	99, 110	
Farmer, Kyle	99	
Finnegan, Brandon	95	
Friedl, T.J.	99, 109	
Garcia, Jose	99, 108	
Garrett, Amir	60	
Gennett, Scooter	32	
Gray, Sonny	62	
Greene, Hunter	96, 105	
Gutierrez, Vladimir	97, 107	
Hendrix, Ryan	101	
Herget, Jimmy	101, 110	
Hernandez, David	64	
Hughes, Jared	66	
Iglesias, Jose	34	
Iglesias, Raisel	68	
India, Jonathan	90, 104	
Isabel, Ibandel	99	
Johnson, Sherman	99	
Kemp, Matt	36	
Lorenzen, Michael	70	
Mahle, Tyler	72	
Mella, Keury	74	
O'Grady, Brian	99	
Patterson, Jordan	91	
Peralta, Wandy	76	
Peraza, Jose	38	
Puig, Yasiel	40	
Rainey, Tanner	111	
Reed, Cody	78	
Reyes, Jesus	101	
Richardson, Lyon	101, 110	
Roark, Tanner	80	
Rodriguez, Alfredo	99	
Romano, Sal	82	
Santillan, Tony	98, 106	
Schebler, Scott	42	
Senzel, Nick	92, 103	
Siani, Mike	99, 106	
Sims, Lucas	84	
Siri, Jose	93, 108	
Stephens, Jackson	101	
Stephenson, Robert	101	
Stephenson, Tyler	99, 109	
Suarez, Eugenio	44	
Trahan, Blake	99	
Trammell, Taylor	94, 104	

Cincinnati Reds 2019

Varner, Seth	101	Winker, Jesse	50
Votto, Joey	46	Wisler, Matt	86
Williams, Mason	48	Wood, Alex	88

Ballpark diagrams for Baseball Prospectus are created by THIRTY81Project, a design concept offering original ballpark artwork, including the new 'Ballparks of 2019' 11 x 17 color print.

Visit **www.thirty81project.com** for full details.

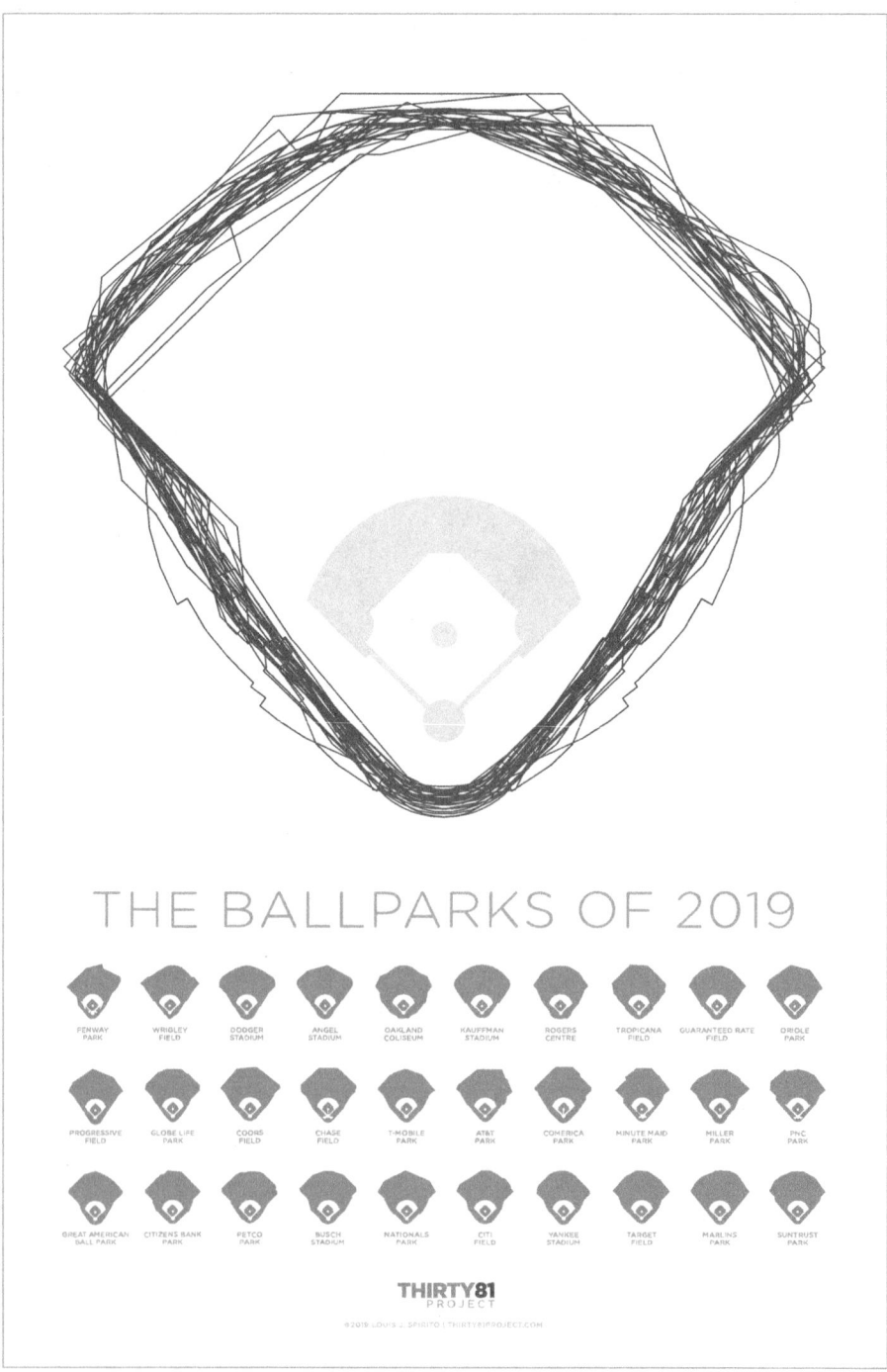